Spitfire

John Vader

Pan/Ballantine

Editor-in-Chief: Barrie Pitt
Art Director: Peter Dunbar

Military Consultant: Sir Basil Liddell Hart
Picture Editor: Robert Hunt

Executive Editor: David Mason
Designer: John Marsh
Cover: Denis Piper
Research Assistant: Yvonne Marsh
Special Drawings: John Batchelor

Photographs for this book were specially selected from the following Archives: from left to right page 2-3 Imperial War Museum; 7 'Wing Leader' by Johnnie Johnson, published by Chatto & Windus 1956; 9 IWM; 10 IWM; 13 Flight International; 14 Flight International; 15 Flight International; 17 Flight International/Ministry of Defence, Air Dept./Flight International; 18-19 Flight International; 22 Ministry of Defence, Air Dept./'The Aeroplane'; 23 Flight International; 24-25 IWM; 28 IWM/Flight International; 31 IWM; 32-33 'The Aeroplane'; 35 'The Aeroplane'; 36 'The Aeroplane'; 37 IWM; 40-41 'The Aeroplane'; 44 IWM; 45 Keystone; 46-47 Keystone; 49 IWM; 50-51 IWM; 54 IWM; 55 IWM; 56 IWM/Keystone; 58-59 IWM; 61 IWM/Keystone; 62 Flight International; 63 Sado Opera Mundi; 64-65 Central Press; 67 IWM; 68 IWM; 69 IWM; 70-71 IWM; 73 IWM; 74 IWM; 76 Sado Opera Mundi; 77 IWM; 78 United Press International; 79 'The Times'/Radio Times Hulton Picture Library; 82 IWM/Keystone; 84 IWM; 89 IWM/US Navy; 92-93 Flight International; 95 IWM; 96 Keystone; 97 Keystone; 98-99 IWM; 100 IWM; 102 IWM; 105 IWM; 106 Canadian Armed Forces; 107 IWM; 109 IWM; 110 IWM; 111 IWM; 112 IWM/US Air Force; 114-115 IWM; 116 IWM; 117 IWM; 118 Vickers Ltd; 121 IWM; 123 Ministry of Defence, Air Dept.; 124-125 Keystone; 127 IWM/Keystone; 128 Radio Times Hulton Picture Library; 130 IWM; 136 IWM; 138-139 IWM; 140 IWM; 141 IWM; 143 IWM; 145 IWM; 146-147 Flight International; 148 Flight International; 149 IWM; 151 IWM; 152 IWM; 155 IWM; 156 IWM.

First U.S. Printing: October, 1969
First Pan/Ballantine Printing: August, 1972

Printed in the United States of America
Ballantine Books, Ltd.—An Intertext Publisher
Pan Books, Ltd.
33 Tothill Street, London, S.W. 1

Contents

The Thoroughbred

Introduction by Air Vice-Marshal 'Johnnie' Johnson

Air fighting began in 1914 when squadrons of the Royal Flying Corps flew to France and scouted for our Army. The slow two-seater machines were unarmed, but pilots and observers usually carried rifles or revolvers to defend themselves should they be forced down. Sometimes they saw German aeroplanes also making reconnaissances, and there began a crude form of duelling in the air when speeds did not exceed seventy miles an hour. In these early clashes there was a sense of sharing the same sport, which made a man hesitate to finish a crippled opponent; but later this affinity between opposing airmen disappeared.

The next step was to arm the two-seaters with machine guns, but as the air fighting intensified there was a requirement for fast single-seat scouts to protect the reconnaissance machines and to seek the enemy on fighting patrols. Lone scout pilots soon found that they could not completely protect themselves from a surprise attack and they began to fly and fight in pairs. Soon pairs developed into sections of four scouts, sections into squadrons, and squadrons into wings until, towards the end of the First War, the Germans operated 'circuses' of fifty vividly painted scouts.

Between the wars both sides forgot a lot of the hard-won tactical lessons, but the Spanish Civil War served to remind the Luftwaffe of the basic rules of air fighting, and German fighter pilots were far better prepared than their RAF contemporaries for the 1939–45 contest, when our stupid peacetime training cost us dear. The author describes these rigid regulation attacks which curbed initiative and forfeited surprise – the very essence of air fighting tactics. Fortunately, young and able leaders, especially Douglas Bader and the great South African pilot, 'Sailor' Malan, did more than anyone else to get our fighting tactics right, and it says much for the RAF's 'family' system of command that these squadron leaders and wing commanders were able to get their views across to our senior commanders, Leigh-Mallory and Keith Park.

In Fighter Command the leadership, from squadron commander to group commander, was excellent and the knowledge that we had good, approachable and understanding senior commanders – who spoke our language – gave us added confidence and increased our morale. On the other hand our German adversaries had little regard for their commander-in-chief, Hermann Göring, and their

iets sparked and flashed over (if you were lucky) the top of the cockpit. You 'broke' into a steep, tight turn to face the attack and asked your Spitfire for everything. For manoeuvrability to out-turn your enemies. For power to try and gain precious height, or to make your escape. For reliable guns and cannon to fight back. Rarely did she fail you.

As a defensive fighter it was unanimously agreed, by fighter pilots of many nationalities, that Reginald Mitchell's immortal Spitfire was superior to any other Allied or enemy fighter. There were occasions when the Germans possessed a decided advantage, and I am thinking especially of 1942 when the Focke-Wulf 190s gave our Spitfire Vs a very hard time. However, this disadvantage was redressed with the best Spitfire of them all, the Spitfire IX, which was such a delight to fly. Again, in late 1944 the Germans caught us unawares with their jets, especially the Messerschmitt 262, and had the fighter version of this fine aeroplane been produced in quantity then we might well have lost our hard-won air superiority over north-west Europe.

Fortunately, for us, Hitler himself ruled that the Messerschmitt 262 was to be developed as a bomber, and so it was that when we invaded Normandy variants of Mitchell's basic Spitfire design swept unchallenged from the Elbe to Normandy. Previously, she had harassed the Afrika Korps from El Alamein to Tunisia. She had duelled out of fortress Malta, and had patrolled the Bay of Bengal.

Men came from every corner of the free world to fly and fight in Spitfires. Men from countries where freedom had a meaning in their minds. A babel of tongues chattered in her cockpit, and all came to love her for her thoroughbred qualities.

Today there are only a handful of Spitfires still flying, and seldom can be heard that nostalgic whistling call as she arcs across the sky. But occasionally, after all these years, I am privileged to fly in that familiar cockpit again when the song of her Merlin engine brings back a hundred memories of those valiant years.

experienced fighter leaders, like Adolf Galland and Werner Molders, were often dismayed and baffled by his ever-changing orders. Indeed, Göring's faulty judgement materially helped us win the Battle of Britain.

Throughout the Second World War the key to air fighting was teamwork. We Spitfire pilots lived, played, trained and fought together. Our fighter leaders always tried to launch a coordinated attack against the Messerschmitts and Focke-Wulfs so that the greatest number of guns were brought against the enemy formation. But once combat was joined it was impossible to hold the team together because of our high speeds and constant manoeuvring. After the initial attack wings and squadrons were soon split up, and although we were taught that a pair of Spitfires was the smallest fighting unit – because no individual could guard his own tail – we often found ourselves alone against enemy fighters.

Most fighter pilots knew the swift, almost unbelievable transformation from the confused hurly-burly of the dog-fight to the dangerous solitude of a seemingly empty sky. For the lone pilot this was the time of great peril when the yellow-nosed Messerschmitts dived from the sun, fastened on your tail, and the wicked tracer bul-

Prologue

On the ground a Spitfire is surprisingly small, balancing delicately on wheels seemingly too close together, with a tiny, cluttered cockpit and very thin wings. At least, this is how it impressed pilots trained on Harvards and making their first close inspection of the fighter; it did not express the 'spitting fire' image of a Battle of Britain winner. Standing, engine stopped, it had a graceful, sculptural form of movement, of flight temporarily suspended; in flight, its shape altered constantly as it moved through varying profile and plan positions, but was always attractive. Like all aircraft, it had its own individual smell made up of the metals, fabrics, paints, oil and fuel, a mixture which the pilot could always smell as he sat in the cockpit. To Spitfire-ambitious pilots, this aircraft was the most beautiful thing on earth.

Entrance to the cockpit is made from the port side – the side cavalry-men mount their horses. The pilot first steps on to the rear of the wing a couple of feet from the ground, then steps with the right leg first into the cockpit. The perspex canopy has to be pushed right back and a flap in the side of the fuselage below the canopy in the metal skinning dropped down on its hinges. The parachute which the pilot is wearing low slung becomes his cushion as he sits in the bucket seat, which is fixed in the raised position until the aircraft is airborne. Now that he is sitting in the cockpit the pilot finds it more comfortable than he might have expected and that the instruments and controls are sensibly and conveniently arranged.

The cockpit drill before starting up is quite simple – oxygen tube attached to the face mask, radio plugged in and switched to the right channel, brakes hard on, throttle open about a third of the way forward, a couple of pumps on the Ki-gas knob (to prime the engine) and thumbs up to the aircraftsman standing by the battery cart from which electrical leads are attached to the starter, in order to save the aircraft's own battery for emergency starts. Once the motor bursts into life, the throttle is brought back to idling position, the chocks are removed from in front of the wheels and, with a little throttling forward,

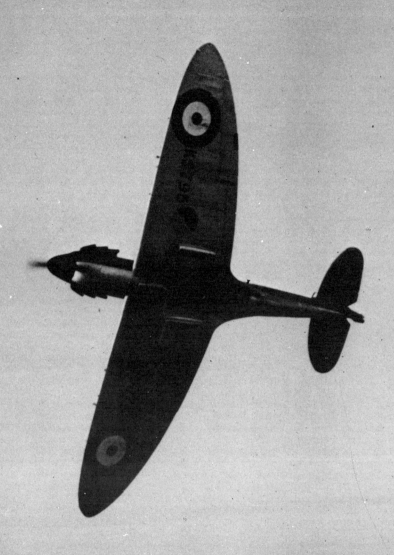

A prewar Spitfire I shows off its
lines in a bank to starboard

A parade-ground 'vic' of Spitfire Is

the Spitfire is taxied to the take-off position on the field. Pilots during the war were taught a code for remembering the check list for starting and taking off: the letters BTFCPPUR – brakes, trims, flaps, contacts, petrol, pressures, undercarriage and radiator, and this list is still used for the surviving aircraft. After some practice the checking and adjusting is performed almost automatically.

When the aircraft reaches the downwind end of its take-off run, it is turned into wind, the Merlin is revved up to test the two magnetoes –too big a drop in engine revolutions when one is turned off is sufficient to cancel the flight. Turning the aircraft while taxiing is effected by pressure on the rudder pedals, while the pilot at the same time releases the pneumatic pressure to the brakes by moving a lever attached to the circular handle of the control column. Finally the brakes are fully released and the throttle and pitch controls are pushed forward, the pitch to fully-fine immediately, the throttle slowly at first, so as to avoid choking the engine,

with the stick held slightly back; the torque of the airscrew, as engine revolutions build up, tends to pull the aircraft to starboard and this has to be counteracted by pressure on the left rudder pedal; the long nose blocks the view in front of the aircraft until the fast-gathering speed of wind over the elevators gives them sufficient 'bite' to make them effective, then the stick is eased forward and the tail is raised, slowly and carefully because the tips of the airscrew blades spin very close to the ground when take-off attitude, with the tail high, has been reached.

With the propeller in fine pitch the engine at full throttle is now making its characteristic sound, a loud, throbbing, burring roar; the aircraft quickly reaches flying speed and without looking at the tachometer the pilot can feel the willingness of the aircraft to take off, and the stick is gently eased back.

As it leaves the ground, the Spitfire is flying at about 100 mph, the speed increasing as the stick is pulled back a little more with the right hand (the left is on the knobs of the throttle and pitch levers) and then to the left, with some pressure on left rudder to make a climbing turn to port. The usual pattern for 'circuit and bumps' – take-offs and landings – and for all service flying is a left-hand circuit (anti-clockwise) round the airfield. The wheels have been retracted soon after leaving the ground, the left hand lifting a lever controlling the pneumatic operation, an indicator showing when they are locked. The revs are reduced and engine boost brought back to its setting for the climb to the desired altitude.

By now, the pilot has experienced the fine sensitivity of the Spitfire, finer than that of a Harvard or even a Hurricane, but closer to that possessed by the delicate Tiger Moth. The pilot continually checks the air speed indicator (ASI), the rev counter, the engine boost gauge and oil and petrol pressure gauges, oil and radiator temperature gauges, compass heading and altimeter. He has closed the radiator and the hood and is climbing for height, after trimming the elevator tabs to ease the pressure on the stick; every marked change of speed varies the pressures on the elevators – the faster the aircraft flies, the more the elevators tend to rise and so make the aircraft climb unless the small trimming tab is adjusted by means of the wheel in the cockpit to neutralise this tendency; for slower speeds, the tabs are trimmed in the opposite direction. Above 10,000 feet, where the oxygen is turned on and its flow registered on a meter, the Spitfire is dived and pulled up for a loop, a half-roll off the top of the loop, some steep turns, slow rolls, a stall and a spin to test control responses.

The stalls are tame, at about 70 mph, and are not vicious, giving plenty of warning shudders – the Spitfire prefers to fly than fall. As he lands on an airstrip, the pilot flies down the right side of the strip, watching the control tower for the green light. At the end he turns to port then turns to port again, flying downwind, lowers his undercarriage and flaps and, at about 500 feet, at the end of this downwind 'leg', he opens his radiator, to keep engine coolant temperature down in compensation for the slower speed of the aircraft as it lands. He then turns again to port, opens his canopy, raises his seat and begins a spiral turn down to the strip, his engine throttled back but with the revs high enough for him to open up the engine to full power quickly if he has to go round the circuit again if he under-shoots or overshoots the runway. During the turn the pilot has a good view of his landing path and as he straightens up the aircraft is only about twenty or thirty feet above the ground and takes up a tail-down attitude for a three-point landing. If there is not much wind the Spitfire seems to float on and on; it sinks down eventually and as throttle and stick are pulled back at the same time the Spitfire stalls one inch above the ground and all three wheels touch down together. (It happens to some the first time, to others very rarely.)

The rudder begins to lose some of its bite and the brakes, first one, then the other, under gentle pressure on the pneumatic system, have to control the landing run. When it has slowed down enough the Spitfire turns to taxi back to its dispersal area, swinging from side to side to 'clear its nose' (let the pilot see round the nose) and avoid obstacles, brakes are applied and locked on, the engine is given a quick rev up, the throttle lever is pulled back and the switches are turned off. The landing could have been rougher, could have been dropped in from a few feet (the oil and air suspension of the Spitfire would have been severely tested, but not broken, although a drop from twelve feet would have done some damage). The Spitfire's toughness is incredible for such a small and frail-looking aircraft that was virtually a first transition from biplanes and was bred for speed through an ancestry of floatplanes; its toughness was an inspiration to the nervous. Spitfires have hit the ground, touched the sea, bashed through trees, cut telegraph and high tension wires, collided in the air, been shot to pieces, had rudders and parts of wings fall off and have yet made safe landings, with or without wheels. Reginald Mitchell designed the Spitfire to be superior to any known fighter in the world at the time but he also made sure that it was a safe plane to fly.

Schneider Trophy and prototype

Reginald Joseph Mitchell was born on 20th May, 1895, in the village of Talke, near Stoke-on-Trent, Staffordshire. His father was a teacher, a school head-master, who later founded a printing business at Hanley, Stoke-on-Trent. When Reginald Mitchell finished his high school education he was appren-ticed, at the age of seventeen, to the Kerr, Stewart & Co locomotive works at Stoke. The steam transport age was in its glorious post-Edwardian period when aeroplane pilots would hire a train to follow them with fuel and mechanics on cross-country races. It was also a blossoming period for aero-planes, irresistible to young, imagin-ative engineers like Mitchell who soon started to design and build flying models in his spare time. Geniuses were at work – Henry Royce was building and Charles Rolls selling beautifully engineered, fast and silent cars; in America, Henry Ford was manufacturing the utilitarian and reliable Model T that sold for a song: the years before the First World War were the beginning of man's greatest age of mechanical invention and young Mitchell threw himself into it

body and soul, studying engineering, mechanics, higher mathematics and drawing at night school. At home he installed a lathe in his bedroom to test theory with practice.

When the First World War broke out, his trade precluded him from ser-vice and he stayed with the firm until he completed his basic training in 1916. The following year he jumped at the opportunity to work as assistant to Hubert Scott-Paine, chief engineer and designer at the Supermarine Aviation Works at Woolston on the Itchen river near Southampton. (The company had been founded in 1912 by Noel Pemberton-Billing, a pioneer aviator who built his first flying-boat, the 'PB 1' in 1913.) He married in 1918 and contentedly settled down in Southampton where he lived and worked for the rest of his life. In 1920, Scott-Paine appointed Mitchell chief engineer and designer on projects mainly concerned with military flying boats.

The First World War had given the world's aircraft industries enormous impetus and once peace had been re-established, aero clubs fostered com-

Mitchell and Royce, parents of the
Schneider Trophy racers and Spitfire

petition and development. In Britain, the Royal Aero Club was eminent in organising aeronautical competitions and British entrants flew in the Gordon Bennett Race for landplanes and competed for the Deutch Cup. On 5th December 1912, Jacques Schneider, son of a French armaments magnate, was a guest at an Aero Club of France banquet in Paris, a banquet where champagne flowed freely and the air-mad members discussed the wondrous speed of machines of the air. During the course of the evening Jacques Schneider, possibly glowing with champagne, magnanimously offered a trophy, valued at one thousand pounds, to be flown for in international competition, adding a further prize of one thousand pounds to be distributed each year for three years to the winners and runners-up; these were worthwhile prizes for small plane-makers in 1912 when an aircraft could be built for a few hundred pounds and as little as fifty pounds with a second-hand engine. By 1931, governments who desired to back entrants would be faced by an expenditure of millions of pounds. By the end of 1942 the Schneider armaments works would be a heap of rubble after several visits by RAF Lancaster bombers and Jacques Schneider would have died in poverty.

Like the 'Flying Lady' emblem decorating the radiator caps of Rolls-Royce cars, the design of the Schneider Trophy itself reflects the art-nouveau style of the period – the bronze casting shows a winged female figure of Speed kissing a surfing Zephyr recumbent on a breaking wave. The first compe-tition for the Trophy was organised by the Aero Club of France and was one of several events on the programme for the Hydro-Aeroplane competitions flown during 3rd/16th April 1913. As a safety precaution it was decided that the high-speed flights for the Trophy should be open only to seaplanes which could make forced landings anywhere on the open water at Mon-aco, where the competition was held. Part of the competition included a flotation test to prove that the air-craft could remain afloat unattended for six hours, and a test to examine the aeroplane's ability to taxi on the water. It was also decided that up to three aircraft could be entered under

Hubert Scott-Paine, the Supermarine designer who first realised Mitchell's potential

The Schneider Trophy, the object of so much expense, time and trouble, which paved the way for the Spitfire

the sponsorship of each of the official clubs, and the club winning the Trophy in three consecutive contests would become its absolute owner. Each succeeding contest was to be organised by the current Trophy holders and the course was not to be less than 150 nautical miles, either in a straight or broken line or in a closed circuit.

There were only four entrants in the first race on 16th April 1913 – three French and one American – a slow and unspectacular race won by Maurice Prevost flying a Deperdussin at an average speed of 45.75 mph. The event was not planned as a race in the true sense although some planes were overtaken; competitors took off at intervals for a race against the clock. Prevost's time would have been better had he not omitted to cross the finishing line and wasted another hour on an extra flight to do so. Apart from flying enthusiasts it is doubtful if many other people in the world took much notice of the event. The following year the contest was held again at Monaco, the winner being a British Sopwith flown by C Howard Pixton at an average speed of 86.78 mph. Pixton later enlivened the aeronautical world by establishing a world seaplane record of 92 mph. The French were pleased that the Sopwith's engine was a Gnôme rotary made in France.

The war precluded any further racing and in 1919 fog closed in on the Royal Aero Club's Bournemouth course where the only aircraft to fly the distance through the murk was an Italian, generously awarded the

Trophy despite the pilot, Janello, having missed one of the turning points. The contest was anulled, however, although the Italian club was asked to hold the competition in 1920 despite this. The venue was Venice where Liugi Bologna won for Italy in a Savoia at an average speed of 107.224 mph. In the following year, again at Venice, Signor G di Briganti won the Trophy in a Macchi at an average speed of 110.84 mph. In both of these contests the Italians won by a 'fly-over', as they were the only competitors to start: no British aircraft had been entered and a Frenchman, the only other entrant in the second race, crashed before the start. If the 1919 race had not been ruined by fog, Italy would have been the official victors and won three in a row by 1921 to keep the Trophy and end the series.

One of Mitchell's first aircraft was the Martlesham Amphibian, built in 1920; this combined structural strength with refined lines, two qualities which were always a hallmark of his designs. The Martlesham was powered by a Rolls-Royce Eagle VIII with pusher propeller, won an eight thousand pound government prize and in an improved military version, was ordered by the Royal Air Force and Royal Australian Air Force. A few were still flying in 1941.

Supermarine decided to enter the Schneider Trophy competitions and for the 1922 event Mitchell and Scott-Paine collaborated, aided by a team of six or seven draughtsmen and tracers, to develop a racing flying boat powered by a 450 hp Napier Lion engine driving a pusher propeller. The Supermarine Sea Lion II, as it was called, was fully aerobatic and could be stunted in the same way as a fighter. It had a stepped hull and was amphibian, although the wheels were stripped from it for the race. The Sea Lion II was taken to Naples and successfully prevented the Italians from claiming the Trophy permanently. Flown by C Biard over a 230-mile course, it flew at an average speed of 145.7 mph, defeating the Italians by a narrow margin. This contest was given more publicity than previous Trophy contests and the world's press began to take a more lively interest in the seaplane races.

Now it was Britain's turn to lay out a course which the Royal Aero Club chose and laid out at Cowes in the Isle of Wight. The American government entered this competition with a Curtiss C.R.3 Navy Racer piloted by Lieutenant David Rittenhouse who took the Trophy at a speed of 177.38 mph, the American seaplane bettering the time made by Britain's Sea Lion III flying boat by 26.22 mph. After this defeat at the hands of the American floatplane Mitchell realised that the floatplane was potentially faster than the flying boat, and determined to devote his energies to producing a floatplane series capable of winning the Trophy outright for Britain.

In 1924 there was no contest for lack of entries and in 1925 a neat little Curtiss biplane on twin floats carried off the prize, flown this time by Lieutenant James Doolittle as an Army Racer at an average speed of 232.57 mph. For this contest, held at Baltimore, Supermarine and Napier each financed a new aircraft and its engine. It was Mitchell's design, a break away from the biplane and boat-hull formula to a mid-wing monoplane seaplane on twin floats and was called the S.4 – the fourth Supermarine Trophy machine. Steel tubes formed the central structure to which were attached a one-piece wing, the fuselage and floats, all of wood construction, and the 700 hp Napier engine. The S.4, flown by Biard, had set a world speed record of 226.75 mph and was expected to bring home the Trophy. The seaplane unfortunately made a crash-alighting during the elimination trials, however, and sank, Biard swimming up from the bottom. Bert Hinkler, famous for his solo flight to Australia, flew a replacement Gloster-Napier III which failed to complete the tests in time. The remaining British entrant, another Gloster-Napier III, flown by Hubert Broad, flew into second place behind James Doolittle's Curtiss R3C-2. The ancestor to the Spitfire had got away to a poor start and was already showing a strong aversion to water. In 1925, Mitchell had also built the large Southampton flying boat, a military version of his 1924 Swan amphibian, a twin-engined biplane on a large wooden hull.

There was no British entrant in the Schneider Trophy contest of 1926 when the world speed record was again raised and Major Mario de Bernadi flew his Macchi M.39 around the Hampton Broads course at an average of 246.44 mph, winning the Trophy for the Italian aero club. The new high speeds and temperamental one-race-only engines caused Mitchell concern for his pilots; he trusted his design and workmanship but was aware of the perils of flying in those days and devoted much attention to making his aircraft as safe as he could.

By 1927, the cost of preparing several aircraft for the Trophy was beyond the resources of single manufacturers and as the development resulting from the competition was of national interest the British government provided funds and assistance to aircraft makers. Gloster, Short and Supermarine were the main contenders for the honour of representing the Royal Aero Club in Italy. Mitchell's ambition was now definitely aimed at winning the Trophy outright. His S.5 was a low-wing monoplane with streamlined wires bracing the wings to the fuselage and floats, the wooden wings carrying water-cooling radiators on their surface, a system which reduced drag, and long channels on the all-metal, oval, monocoque fuselage holding the oil-cooling pipes for the same reason. Fuel was carried in the metal floats, a greater proportion in the starboard float to help maintain balance against the torque of the 900 hp Napier Lion engine. Wing span was 26 feet 9 inches, wing area 115 square feet, length 24 feet 1 inch, weight 3,250 pounds, maximum speed 320 mph and landing speed 90 mph.

The Royal Navy carried the two S.5s, three Gloster IVs and one Short Crusader, in the aircraft carrier HMS *Eagle* to Venice where the contest was held off the Lido, outside the Lagoon and over the open Adriatic. Seven laps

Top: **The Supermarine Sea Lion, winner of the 1922 Schneider Trophy.** *Centre:* **The S.4, first of Mitchell's monoplane racers.** *Right:* **S.5, two of which finished first and second in the 1927 race**

Supermarine S.6B N 247, victor of the
1929 Schneider Trophy race off
Spithead

were to be flown over a triangular course of fifty kilometres (thirty-one miles) with two hairpin bends where the pilots would be subjected to black-outs due to gravity forces in the steep turns. The American entrant (which had flown at 322 mph to establish a world record) was not ready in time, the Italians entered three Macchi-Fiat M.52s, and Britain entered two S.5s and a Gloster IVB. The S.5s were the only two aircraft to complete the course, the faster averaging 281.656 mph flown by Flight-Lieutenant S N Webster, RAF.

The Schneider Trophy was by now the world's major aeronautical event, with Britain, Italy and America as the most interested contenders. Because of the time, and cost, required to prepare the racing seaplanes, the *Fédération Aeronautique Internationale* (FAI), which had taken over control of the contest, ruled that the Trophy event should be flown every two years instead of annually. Thus it was not until 1929 that Britain could be host country and provide a course, at Spithead on the mainland opposite the Isle of Wight, of fifty kilometres (thirty-one miles) laid out in quadrilateral form. The French entrant withdrew, the American aeroplane was damaged in preliminary trials, the Italians entered three Macchis – an M52 and two M67s – and the British could choose from two Gloster IVs, two Supermarine S.6s and one S.5.

Flying any of these machines required a higher skill than for any Second World War or modern aircraft. The pilots flew what were virtually experimental types at very high speeds, the powerful motors and flimsy wings making taxiing, take-off and alighting very awkward, and the controls requiring brute strength for some manoeuvres in flight. The view from the open cockpits was poor and, after alighting very fast, up to two miles of water were crossed before the aircraft came to a stop. Many Trophy aircraft from all the competing countries crashed in test flights and trials during the contest years, contributing their share of noise, glamour and danger to the 'Roaring Twenties'. Pilots in the RAF High Speed Flight included H R D Waghorn, R L R Atcherley, G H Stainforth, d'Arcy

Grieg and A H Orlebar. Flying Officer Waghorn won the 1929 contest for Britain, attaining a top speed of 370 mph and an average of 328.63 mph in his S.6.

The S.6 seaplane, marked by the long oil cooling ducts on the side of the fuselage, was powered by a motor different to that of the S.5. When Mitchell chose the Rolls-Royce V12 water-cooled 1,900 hp engine for the S.6, it was the beginning of a non-stop marriage between his aircraft (racers and future fighters) and Rolls-Royce engines. The Buzzard had been developed by Henry Royce and A J Rowledge from the banked-V Eagle engine for which Royce had made his first drawings in 1914 and from which basic constructional form would emerge the famous Merlin. The Eagle was the first Rolls-Royce aero engine, going into production in 1915, and Eagles powered the Vickers Vimy bomber which was the first aircraft to fly the Atlantic non-stop in 1919. The Air Ministry had followed the progress at Rolls-Royce closely and had recommended Mitchell to examine the hotted-up Buzzard when he was looking for something with greater power than the 1,400 hp Napier. The improved Buzzard was dubbed 'R' – for Racing – and after the decision to produce it for Mitchell's racers had been made in February 1929, Rolls-Royce invested months of intensive work to have it ready in time for the 1929 contest; at nearly two thousand horse power, the engine had a 'life' of at least one hour at full throttle!

The world depression of the late 1920s seriously restricted government expenditure in Britain and no funds were available from that source for Supermarine to produce an aircraft for the 1931 Schneider Trophy contest. Then, just in time, a million-airess patriot, Lady Houston, gave £100,000 so that Supermarine and Rolls-Royce could produce the S.6B – a development of the S.6 rather than a new design, as there were only seven months before the contest was due to be flown. Without Lady Houston's gift, the Spitfire would have eventually evolved, but by preparing the S.6B in 1931, Mitchell gained valuable experience more quickly. He modified two S.6s and built two new S.6Bs

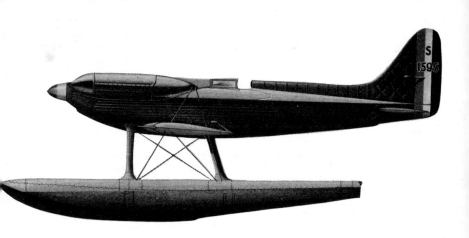

Supermarine S.6B
Engine: Rolls-Royce 'R', 2,300 hp *Maximum speed:* This aircraft won the
1931 Schneider Trophy race at 340.08 mph *Weight empty:* 4,590 lbs
Weight loaded: 6,086 lbs *Span:* 30 feet 0 inches *Length:* 28 feet 10 inches

powered by the 'R'. Rolls-Royce engineers boosted power by twenty-one per cent with a weight increase of only seven per cent; bore was six inches, stroke six and a half inches, capacity 2,240 cubic inches (36.7 litres), weight 1,640 lbs, compression ratio 6:1, and fuel consumption an incredible 180 gallons per hour. Fuel was a blend of benzole and petrol. Without changing its size, 400 hp was added to the engine.

The FAI had decided that entrants should comply with more stringent regulations aimed at improving the reliability of aircraft: a preliminary trial was held as part of the main contest, each aircraft had to take off, ascend to 150 feet, alight, taxi for two minutes, take off again and then fly past the starting point. This meant that each aircraft carried more fuel than in any previous contest. Fuel for the S.6Bs was carried in the float opposite the one which took the strain of torque so that the plane could be taxied without ploughing into the sea.

Italian and French clubs nominated their competitors but on the day the British machines were unopposed, and it was only necessary for one to fly the seven laps of the fifty kilometre triangular course off Spithead. Flight-Lieutenant J N Boothman uneventfully completed the rounds in his S.6B at an average speed of 340.08

mph. The Schneider Trophy, symbolising more than any other monument the rapid development from clumsy biplanes to sleek monoplanes, was permanently in Britain's possession, due to the endeavours of Mitchell, Rolls-Royce, the RAF and Lady Houston. The Trophy now graces the ante-room of the Royal Aero Club in Piccadilly.

On 13th September 1931, Flight-Lieutenant G H Stainforth established a world speed record in an S.6B. The amazing 'R' was boosted yet again (to 2,550 hp) and powered the Mitchell aircraft to another world speed record of 407 mph. The 'R' was also used in record-breaking speedboats piloted by Sir Henry Seagrave, Kaye Don and Sir Malcolm Campbell, and two powered the Thunderbolt car which George Eyson drove at 312 mph in 1937.

In those halcyon days of leisured flight with struts and wires humming between wood and fabric wings, it was a tremendous advance in the evolution of the aeroplane when a designer of braced biplanes built fast, canti-levered-wing monoplanes. Reginald Mitchell (he was called 'R J' by all and sundry at Supermarine) combined sound knowledge with rare inspiration to comprise the aeronautical engineering that went into his 1931 contest winner. He made use of wind tunnel tests and observed the developments made by his competitors' aircraft, quickly adopting and improving whatever innovations the world or aeronautics could offer. He was appointed to a directorship of Supermarine in 1928, the year he was awarded the Royal Aeronautical

Below: Final victor in the Schneider Trophy series – the S.6B S 1595.
Bottom: S.6B S 1596, which raised the speed record to 379.05 mph in 1931. *Right and far right:* two men always associated with the S.6Bs, Flight-Lieutenants Boothman and Stainforth, race winner and record breaker

Society's Silver Medal; he was made a Fellow of the Society in 1929, honoured by the King with the award of Commander of the Order of the British Empire (CBE) in 1931 and would certainly have been awarded higher honours had he lived when the Spitfire proved itself in battle.

Sir Henry Royce said of Mitchell that he was slow to decide and quick to act. His main characteristics were an ability for deep concentration – for which he desired absolute non-interruption – and a notable capacity for leadership combined with enthusiastic support for unconventional ideas from his designers and engineers. He

played tennis, cricket and golf, and was a football club supporter; he qualified as a pilot and enjoyed flying about the countryside in a Tiger Moth. He was what might be described as a typical Englishman, pipe-smoking and tweed-suited, good natured, somewhat shy and possessing a good sense of humour. He nevertheless demanded and received from his employees a high standard of work. As chief engineer and designer he produced twenty-four different types of aircraft between 1920 and 1936: bombers, flying boats, amphibians, racing seaplanes, light aeroplanes and two interceptor fighters.

In 1928 the Supermarine company had been taken over by Vickers (Aviation) Ltd, a branch of the firm famous as builders of warships, tanks and guns. Vickers were interested in the production of flying boats, a neglected sphere of aeronautics at the time, and so the design and construction of such types became Mitchell's prime occupation for most of his working life. While creating racing seaplanes he continued to build flying boats, and four examples of one of his most outstanding designs, South-ampton Mk IIs, made a remarkable flight of twenty-three thousand miles in 1927. Led by Group-Captain H N Cave-Brown-Cave, they flew in formation to Basra, Karachi, Calcutta,

through the East Indies, around Australia, to Singapore, Hong Kong and back to Singapore. In 1928, Mitchell built the Solent three-engined flying boat and, in 1929, the Seamew reconnaissance amphibian as well as an 'air yacht' – a three-engined parasol monoplane flying boat with radial engines mounted on the wing's leading edge – for the Hon A E Guinness. Mitchell's Walrus, built as a Royal Navy reconnaissance and air-sea rescue aircraft, was a biplane flying boat that was fully aerobatic and when thrown about in rolls and spins looked like a verandah caught in a whirlwind; it was safe and reliable and a few were still flying in 1948. If Mitchell's versatility in designing flying boats proved him a man of outstanding genius, his Spitfire fighter simply confirmed it.

Although the British government had expended a lot of money on Mitchell's non-military speed floatplanes and were forced to back the venture even further when Lady Houston made her donation, the Air Ministry was not interested in continuing the development of one or two aircraft for speed attempts alone; they wanted fighters and bombers and preferred to invest in the aircraft industry for a more practical return.

Hugh Dowding, who was to become closely associated with the Spitfire, was one of the Royal Air Force's

senior commanders who had fought on the Western Front with the Royal Flying Corps. He was a tall, ascetic, dedicated airman, nicknamed 'Stuffy', respected by his staff and highly regarded by his superiors; it is doubtful if the RAF ever had the services of a better man for two vital jobs which were to come his way. The RAF transfers senior men from post to post, from active flying duties to administration, to give them experience in various commands, and in 1930 Dowding was at the Air Ministry, responsible for supply and research – a position which put him in close association with aircraft designers, engineers, radar scientists, armament manufacturers and politicians. Dowding used research appropriation funds to sponsor experimental bomber and fighter types, yet after Supermarine produced their 400 mph racer, the Air Ministry was prepared to pay for a new fighter with a very modest performance; Supermarine were asked to build an all-metal, four-gun fighter with a short take-off run, low landing

speed and a top speed of 250 mph. In 1930, the Air Ministry wrote a specification (F7/30) for the aircraft, a specification which was a statement of required performance but not of design.

Mitchell designed a rudimentary fighter (the Supermarine Type 224), choosing an untried engine recommended by the Ministry – a steam-cooled Rolls-Royce Goshawk. The aircraft had thick wings, a fixed undercarriage in bulky streamlined spats and protruding nuts on the fuselage; it was sturdy and aerodynamically sound, but could attain only 230 mph when it was completed in 1934. A Scots engineer, Sir Robert McLean, who was chairman of Vickers Aviation and Vickers Supermarine, named the disappointing machine 'Spitfire'.

The Gloster Gladiator, a radial-engined biplane, did satisfy the specification and went into production, while at Supermarine development work progressed on Mitchell's new designs for a better fighter, and non-flying models evolved with retractable undercarriages and enclosed cockpits. Mitchell was aiming at a fighter that was far ahead of those conceived in Ministry specifications. Perhaps the Ministry would have written one for such an aircraft but they were not to know what was in Mitchell's mind

Supermarine F.7/30, the first aircraft to be named Spitfire. It formed an important link between the Schneider Trophy aircraft and the later Spitfire, though it featured a cranked wing

nor how successful Rolls-Royce would be in their efforts to build reliability and long life into an engine of similar size in the 'R'.

Sir Henry Royce had died the year before the spatted, crank-winged Spitfire flew, but before he died he had laid the foundation for the construction of a more practical 'R' design; of about 1,000 hp, for service in RAF aircraft. As a child, Frederick Henry Royce had sold newspapers and worked as a telegraph boy. His father, a poor miller, could not afford to pay for an apprenticeship for his son but an aunt came to the rescue and for twenty pounds a year he was taken on at the Great Northern Railway works at Peterborough at the age of fourteen. Like Mitchell, Royce also had the use of a lathe at his home, a boarding house in Peterborough. He later became interested in electric power and established a business which rapidly became prosperous from the manufacturing of very reliable industrial electric motors. He was caught up by the general enthusiasm for the motor car and built one for himself and one for his partner in the electric motor business. The Hon Charles Rolls, who was in the car selling business at Conduit Street in London's West End, had been very impressed when he inspected the workmanship and observed the quiet, smooth running of Royce's cars. Together they set up business under their joint names. This was the simple beginning of the engineering company (without the electric motor company which Royce continued to operate separately) which was to build the Merlin.

In 1932, a staff of some 600 men in the Rolls-Royce Experimental Department began work on what was to evolve as the most famous aeroplane engine of the war, with over 100,000 built in Britain and the USA and which powered many different types of military aircraft. Construction of the new engine, then known as the PV (Private Venture)-12, required the making of 11,000 pieces, 4,500 of which were not duplicated, as were such parts as pistons, and these were all first turned and carved in hardwood until a model of the whole engine was made entirely in wood, exact in every part. Special metals were tested for use in the valves, which were to work in a temperature of 850 degrees, and in the supercharger impeller which revolved 30,000 times a minute with the rim travelling near the speed of sound. The first engine was ready for test in October, 1934, and was successfully run at full pressure for one hundred hours. It was also tested, and found to

function satisfactorily, at a simulated sub-stratospheric height, where temperatures are 70 degrees below freezing. In April 1935, the PV-12 was test-flown in a Hawker Hart and was also tested in a Heinkel He 70 'Blitz' commercial aircraft purchased in Germany. Mitchell wanted to use this engine for his new Spitfire but it had to undergo further extensive tests before Rolls-Royce were satisfied that it was as reliable as they had planned. Rolls-Royce and the RAF were more than pleased in November 1936 when relays of pilots flew a PV-12 powered Hawker Hart test-bed aircraft for 100 hours spread over eight days: at the end of the test the engine was completely stripped and it proved to be as good as new. It could now be offered to plane makers under its new Rolls-Royce aero engine birds-of-prey series name, Merlin.

Like the Buzzard, the Merlin was adaptable to experiment and development for operating at various heights for peak performances, and for increasing its power output. Its bore (5.4 inches), stroke (6 inches) and capacity (1,657 cubic inches or 27 litres) remained constant throughout its development from 1,030 hp in Merlins I to IV, to over 1,700 hp in the Merlin 64; its length grew slightly from 75.078 inches to 86.212 inches, its height from 41.175 inches to 45.725 inches, while its width remained constant at just under 30 inches. Its long-term power potential was predictable as early as 1938 when a Merlin was give a short-life boost to 2,160 hp.

From the beginning of its production, demand for the Merlin was very high for Spitfire, Hurricane and Boulton-Paul Defiant fighters, Fairey Battle light-bombers and for the new multi-engined bombers. By the time war broke out, Rolls-Royce had stopped car production to concentrate all their resources on the aero engine. To counteract the Germans' fast, low-flying intruders in 1941, the Merlin was boosted forty per cent for extra sea-level power; to reach high-flying enemy fighters the high-rated Merlin 45 was installed in Spitfires and, when the Ju 86P reconnaissance aircraft flew higher still, the Merlin was easily and quickly modified to operate even higher. When the Focke-Wulf 190s

appeared, out-performing current RAF fighters, Rolls-Royce built the Merlin 60 Series engine with a two-stage supercharger and a system for intercooling the air compressed by the supercharger before it went into the cylinders; this supercharging maintained sea-level power in the engine up to 40,000 feet, where the thin air was compressed to six times the pressure of the surrounding atmosphere. Merlins were also manufactured in America; Rolls-Royce sent their detailed drawings to the Packard motor company and thousands of Packard-Merlins were made for use in British and US aircraft.

Instead of continuing with the project for satisfying the F7/30 specification, Supermarine decided to co-operate with Rolls-Royce on the development of Mitchell's new fighter and by the time his ideas were being transformed from drawings into the real aircraft, the Merlin was tested and ready. Mitchell then had a powerful, reliable motor for his new Spitfire – a name Supermarine decided to keep – an aircraft into which he planned to build aerodynamic cleanliness, good flying qualities, strength, speed and fire-power. It was an enormous undertaking: 330,000 man-hours were expended at Supermarine before the Spitfire Mk I went into squadron service. Sadly, the designer himself could spend less and less time on the project for he was beginning to feel the dragging pain and weakening effects of the cancer which was to end his life in 1937.

Perhaps if 'R J' had stopped work or semi-retired in 1933, when he was first operated on, he could have been cured or increased his life span another few years. Instead, he drove himself to work harder in order to build the Spitfire prototype: he had visited Germany and witnessed for himself the Nazi military preparations, he knew of the Heinkel, Dornier and Junkers aircraft and he knew of the Bayerische Flugzeugwerke 109V-I prototype (powered by a Rolls-Royce Kestrel V engine) designed by Willy Messerschmitt. Mitchell felt that he must produce an answer to the German threat, growing month by month in the early 1930s. And, naturally, he had a strong personal wish to see his dream aircraft fly; building the Spitfire was his greatest challenge and he had foreseen its shape and performance long before the jigs had been set up.

Work on the mock-up began as a private venture, as its engine had done, without government backing or any guarantees for orders when it was completed.

During 1935 the prototype Spitfire gradually took shape, its only visual relation to the S.6. being the narrow fuselage. The wings were tapered out to slender tips, had a pretty dihedral and were elliptical. To allow for heavier than usual landings, the undercarriage 'oleo' legs – telescopic-springing on oil and air – were set rather close together, to lower stress on the wings, and swung outward to retract flush into wing cavities; the tail landed on a small skid. As many as thirty propellers were tested until a fixed-pitch two-blade wooden one was chosen; variable-pitch types had not then been perfected but by the time the Battle of Britain was fought the de Havilland three-blade, two-pitch metal propeller was ready. By the end of the war the various marks of Spitfires had necessitated changes to thirteen different types of propellers. A stalling speed of about 70 mph and a landing speed of 85 mph were envisaged. The Merlin 'C' was much less demanding in its cooling needs than the Buzzard – instead of yards of piping running around the fuselage and through the wing surface, there were the two relatively small radiators, the oil radiator under the port wing near the root and the larger radiator, for cooling the glycol which circulated around the cylinders, set back at the rear of the starboard wing root. Glycol, an oily substance, which was used instead of water for engine cooling, boiled at a higher temperature than water; its drawback was that when it did boil it sometimes leaked out of the pipes and produced dangerous fumes that were sucked back into the cockpit and could render a pilot unconscious. It was very difficult indeed to sit head out in the slipstream and land a Spitfire with a glycol leak. Later in the war, when the fighter was not so scarce, pilots were told to bale out rather than risk losing consciousness and crashing with fatal results.

A third orifice protruding beneath the streamlined undersurface of the Spitfire was the carburettor air intake set at the base of the engine nacelle. The stubs of six exhausts were set flush along each side of the engine nacelle, and the cockpit was positioned above the trailing edge of the wings and behind a long nose which would obscure the landing path during the first stage of a take-off and the end of the landing run. The pivot-head for the air speed indicator protruded from the port wing.

At last, twenty months after the first drawings had been started, the prototype was ready to fly, its serial number – K5054 – painted on the light-blue enamelled fuselage. At this stage the prototype Spitfire had official government recognition and a specification had been written for it. Two of the RAF officers who played a major part in the formulation of the specification were Squadron-Leader R S Sorley of the Air Ministry Operational Requirements Branch and Captain F W Hill, the Senior Technical Officer, Ballistics, Martlesham Heath. These two men persuaded the other officers responsible for Specification F37/34 that the new generation of fighters would need eight machine guns firing at the rate of at least 1,000 rounds per minute to destroy the target in the short (two seconds) time that it would be in the sights of the fighter. It was believed that the time would be as short as this because of the fighter's far greater speed. Sorley and Hill had themselves been persuaded of this by tests at the Aeroplane and Armament Experimental Establishment, Martlesham Heath. All of the the latest operational requirements and the best of the previous specifications were incorporated in the specification under which the Spitfire I was finally produced – F16/36. Furthermore, Specification F37/34, issued in January 1935, allowed the government to officially order the construction of the prototype and the 'private' part of the venture ended. On a chilly spring morning, 5th March 1936, Vickers' chief test pilot, J 'Mutt' Summers, took the Spitfire up on its maiden flight, at Eastleigh Airport in Hampshire.

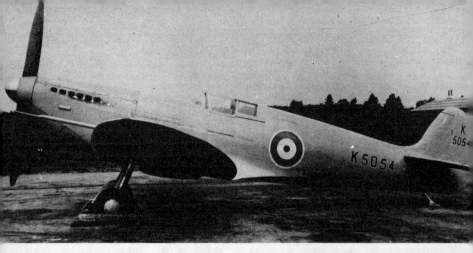

Top: Prototype Spitfire in immaculate pale blue enamel finish.
Above: K 5054 in flight. Note the unbulged canopy and absence of armament. *Left:* Captain J 'Mutt' Summers, the Spitfire's first pilot, pictured in the early 1930s

In test flights it reached 342 mph at 17,000 feet which was very nearly the top speed predicted by 'R J', whose forecasts for top speeds in new models were never out by more than 5 mph. The Type 300, as the aircraft was officially recorded by Supermarine, was first shown to the public at the 1936 Air Display at Hendon, making a strong impression with its perfect lines and apt name.

Mitchell watched his Spitfire climb to the clouds and perform exactly as he had planned. He was very ill but refused to give up his work, although there was little to be done to the Spitfire except the planning for mass production; the machine's design necessitated very few changes and the prototype, K5054, modified to Mk I standard, was still flying in 1940, having survived three crashes. But Mitchell had another project at hand: a bomber just as revolutionary as his fighter, designed to Specification B12/36. The bomber was to be powered by four engines, to have wings with swept-back leading edges and spanning 93 feet, twin main landing and tail wheels, nose and tail power-turrets, a retractable turret amidships, a 370 mph maximum speed, a range of 3,000 miles and a bomb load of 8,000 pounds at this range. Mitchell's bomber was never completed in prototype form – it was destroyed by enemy bombing in 1940 and Supermarine gave up the project to concentrate on Spitfire production.

Reginald Mitchell died in 1937, aged forty-two. He had almost died after the operation in 1933 and when he recovered was much weakened and he never regained his former vigour. He resisted medical advice to give up work after his holiday on the Continent in 1934; what he saw of war preparation there made him determined to provide his country with an outstanding interceptor fighter. Working to finish the fighter and to construct the four-engined bomber eventually took from his body the resistance to the growing cancer, he became very ill and his wife, Florence, took him to a specialist clinic in Austria; it was too late to operate and he was flown home to Southampton where he died soon afterwards. His only child, Gordon, was then seventeen.

Mitchell's illness had not been made public and only his close friends and associates knew the gravity of the disease. His memorials are numerous; the Spitfires preserved in museums and at air force stations throughout the world; the Schneider Trophy representing his pioneering development of flying boats and float planes;

the Mitchell Junior School at Hornchurch, one of the Battle of Britain front line fighter stations, has RAF colours in its pupils' striped ties and blazer badges incorporating the letter M and the outline of a Spitfire; there is a Mitchell Youth Centre at Hanley, Stoke-on-Trent; and there is a feature film on the life of Mitchell and the building of the first Spitfire.

Made in 1942, the film was called 'First of the Few' with the part of Mitchell played by Leslie Howard. In June the following year, Leslie Howard left Lisbon in a Dutch KLM DC3 civil airliner after a long tour of Spain and Portugal. He had been lecturing on behalf of the British Council and encouraging the showing of British documentary and feature films to Spanish and Portuguese audiences; one film was 'Pimpernel Smith' in which he starred as a modern Pimpernel snatching victims from Nazi persecution, a film voted the best of the year by the Portuguese. Howard delayed his departure from Lisbon to attend the local première of 'First of the Few'. Three hours after take-off, in broad daylight, the twin-engined airliner was shot down by eight Ju 88 bombers. There were no survivors nor did the Germans call up their air-sea-rescue aircraft to look for survivors. The take-off times of unarmed airliners flying from Portugal were not hidden from German residents and agents and only two KLM aircraft had been previously attacked. Perhaps Howard's successful propaganda activity and the publicity for the Spitfire annoyed Goebbels, or the Germans may have decided that the civil air communication between Britain and Portugal was detrimental to the war effort of the Axis powers and should be interrupted. Or perhaps a man on the ill-fated airliner looked too much like Winston Churchill – who was then visiting Anthony Eden in Algiers and was due to return to England – a man who wore a bowler hat, smoked cigars and was in fact Howard's business manager, Alfred Chenhalls. Whether or not there was any reason, other than an accidental encounter with a group of trigger-happy Luftwaffe bomber pilots, is a mystery which has yet to be explained.

Into service and training

Before the Spitfire first flew, Air Vice-Marshal Hugh Dowding had been requested to stay beyond his normal tour of duty as Air Member for Supply and Research at the Air Ministry. In 1936, after having watched the development of new fighters and bombers reach a stage where production would flow once the orders were issued, he was given command of Air Defence of Great Britain (ADGB), later known as Fighter Command. The Spitfire had been only one of his department's projects and he was really more interested in bombers but as chief of the country's defence he was to become more closely associated with Spitfires and Hurricanes. As well as interceptor fighters, there were other vital organisations which came under his control at ADGB. There were anti-aircraft regiments of the Army's home defence, searchlights, intelligence, Balloon Command, Observer Corps, the rudimentary radar then gaining acceptance, and the nation's air raid warning network. His headquarters were on the outskirts of London and his immediate requirements were modern fighters and alert warning systems.

With the Spitfire prototype approved and accepted by the Air Ministry, first orders were issued, in June 1936, for the production of 310 Spitfire Is. The Air Ministry was fortunate in having Air-Marshal Wilfred Freeman to carry on from the progressive Dowding; Freeman did as much as any man could with the resources available to get as many fighters as possible from the industry to the airfields, but the machinery of government action and decision was often slow to operate, even in the darkest moments of the war. The requirements for a small, simple fighter with enclosed cockpit and retractable undercarriage, revised for Mitchell's ideas, had also included an armament of eight 0.303 inch machine guns mounted in the wings [see above]. Mitchell had collaborated with Squadron-Leader (later Air-Marshal Sir Ralph) Sorley on armament (the final mock-up conference between the two was on 26th March 1935) and they had decided that a heavy concentration of fire was desirable. Placing so many guns out on the wings was unorthodox but it did away with the necessity of using interrupter gear, which slowed

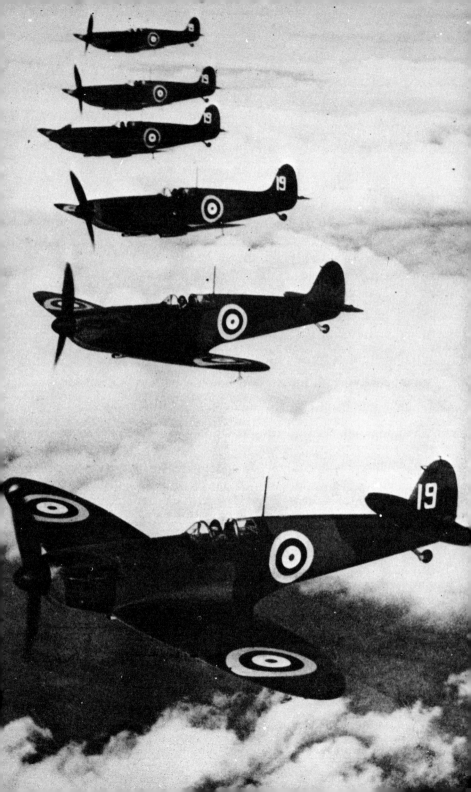

Prewar Mk Is of No 19 Squadron
await an inspection. Note the
two-bladed propellers

the rate of fire, and the extra maintenance required for servicing both gun and gear when they were placed to fire through the disc swept by the propeller. The new American Colt machine gun was chosen as the standard British aircraft machine gun and was installed in the thin Spitfire wings, wings so strong they had achieved in test a Mach number of 0.92. A licence to manufacture the machine gun in Britain was obtained from the Colt Automatic Weapon Corporation of Hartford and the gun was adapted to fire British rimmed cartridges. The gun was enlarged in bore from 0.30 to 0.303 inches and produced under the name of Browning by the Birmingham Small Arms Company. Mitchell's assistant, Joseph Smith, handled the installation of the guns and ammunition bins.

Joseph Smith, FRAeS – and later appointed CBE – succeeded Mitchell as chief designer and engineer for Supermarine. He had been closely associated with the production of the prototype and knew that the basic design was suitable for development, to absorb the greater power and weight of the newer versions of the Merlin then coming into service, and also to bear the weight of the improved propellers necessary to utilise the extra power available. The Spitfire's qualities of speed and efficiency lay in the aerodynamic refinements of a good ratio of low structure weight to high power, and the constant attempts to improve this ratio were as much the responsibility and achievements of the Rolls-Royce technicians as those of Vickers Supermarine. The limit of the Merlin's use was parallel to that of the Spitfire. In 1938 both were a long way from the limit.

The first order for 310 Spitfires was too large for Supermarine to fulfil if they were to manufacture all of the component parts, so orders for three-quarters of the machine, including the wings, were subcontracted to speed production. It actually achieved the reverse result for by the end of 1937 six aircraft were ready except for wings. By March, 1938, the month German troops entered Austria and the Japanese installed a puppet Chinese Republican government at Nanking, only four complete sets of wings were available and Supermarine were forced to make preparations to build their own. The government had been spurred on by events in Europe, North Africa and the Far East to build up the air force, but it was not until 20th June, about four months before the Munich Conference, that the first Spitfire I was tested and ready for delivery to the RAF. By the end of 1938, only forty-nine had been delivered.

The pilots' reception of the Spitfire was ecstatic. After having flown trainers and obsolete biplane fighters, their first flight in the 'Spit', as it was soon commonly called, was exhilarating, many of the pilots returning to earth 'breathlessly excited'. Mutt Summers had raved about the prototype and RAF pilots raved about the Mk I. Their experience could be compared with the riding of a tractable, highly strung thoroughbred after hacking around on a farm horse. The enormous power available did not interfere with the aircraft's delicate, quick and positive response to control movements. By trimming the little elevator tabs to relieve fore and aft pressure on the stick (control column) level flight could be held almost automatically and the plane guided by light hand pressures. With engine stopped, the Spitfire was just as responsive in a 'dead stick' landing, providing an airfield was underneath. The first Spitfire delivered to a fighter squadron (No 19 Squadron at Duxford) was flown more than the others so that the aircraft could be used for maintenance instruction purposes after 240 hours flying, reached in about six weeks.

The Merlin II engine powering the Mk I provided a take-off power of 880 hp and a maximum of 1,030 hp with the throttle pushed through the 'gate' – the thin wire barrier tied across the throttle channels to restrict pilots from using the extra power except in cases of emergency; thus 'emergency power', a phrase often heard in descriptions of combat. 174 Spitfires were fitted with the Merlin II and the rest of the 1,566 Mk Is were fitted with the Merlin III which differed from the Merlin II only in being fitted with an airscrew shaft which was a universal

Prewar line-up of Mk Is belonging to
No 19 Squadron, the first unit to be
equipped with Spitfires

Left: No 19 Squadron again, in one of the prewar formations which was so quickly invalidated *Below:* A Mk I flies in over the south coast while on patrol in the early months of the war

type. The Merlin gave a boost pressure (expressed in pounds per square inch compressed by the supercharger, thus 'pounds of boost') of 6¼ pounds increased by an override of 12 pounds which added speeds of between 5 mph at 18,000 feet to 25 mph at sea level where a top speed of 305 mph was attained, whereas without the override boost the speed would be only 280 mph. At 10,000 feet the 6¼ pounds boost gave 321 mph to which the override added 34 mph. Service ceiling was 31,900 feet and at 30,000 feet the Mk I could fly at 315 mph. It was not as fast as the S.6B speed float plane with its high-powered, limited-life motor but was faster than the prototype; the maximum speed of the Mk I was 362 mph at 18,500 feet. Maximum cruising speed was 315 mph and economical cruising speed 210 mph at 20,000 feet. Maximum range at economical cruising speed was 575 miles; combat range was 395 miles, allowing for take-off and fifteen minutes of combat.

These figures apply to the Mk IA. ('A' suffixed to the mark number of the Spitfire was a retrospective way of indicating that armament comprised eight .303 inch machine guns. This retrospective designation became necessary with the introduction of cannon armament. The next step in armament was the 'B' wing, which had two 20 mm Hispano cannon and four .303 inch machine guns. After this came the 'C' wing, which could accommodate either 'A' or 'B' type armament or a new combination comprising four 20 mm cannon, and which was also known as the 'Universal' wing. Finally there was the 'E' wing, which was designed to accommodate two 20 mm cannon and two .5 inch machine guns. The designation 'D' was not officially allotted.) Except for about thirty which were fitted with 'B' wings, the Supermarine Type 300 Spitfires were Mark IAs in RAF service. When the Mk Is exchanged their wooden propellers for the three-blade, two-pitch de Havilland ones, performance was considerably enhanced, particularly in the climb.

In view of the fact that in 1938 there were several record-breaking planes capable of flying at well over 400 mph, the speeds of the Spitfire were not remarkable. They were, however, very impressive in the world of military aviation where a well-armed fighter capable of climbing to 20,000 feet in 9.4 minutes was highly desirable.

The fuel tanks occupied most of the monocoque fuselage space between the engine and the cockpit. Self-sealing tanks were not installed until 1940. A forty-eight Imperial gallon tank was stacked over a thirty-seven gallon tank – a total capacity of eighty-five gallons of the eighty-seven octane petrol used in the Merlin II and Merlin III. The oil tank was faired to the underneath of the nose beneath the engine and held 5.8 gallons of DTD 109 oil, and the coolant – pure ethylene glycol – was stored in a tank between the engine and the spinner and was cooled by air passing through a large Serck-type radiator, later changed to a Morris car-type secondary-surface radiator fixed under the roof of the starboard wing and opened or closed by using a lever inside the cockpit; the large starboard radiator and the small, circular port oil radiator gave the Spitfires up to Mk VI an asymmetrical appearance when viewed from head on. In place of the six flush engine exhaust ports of the prototype, three exhaust ejectors protruded on either side of the engine, and where the prototype used a landing skid under the tail, the Mk I was equipped with a tailwheel.

As a result of pilots' assessments and further study by both the makers and RAF engineers, improvements continued to be made. The windscreen plastic was replaced with armoured glass, armour plate was fitted at the rear of the engine bulkhead and, while the manually-operated undercarriage pump was retained for use in emergencies, a power-operated pump was installed. The straight cockpit hood of the prototype was replaced by a curved 'blister' type.

In an experiment to find a substitute for metals used in the construction of aircraft fuselages, phenol-resin impregnated flax fibres formed into plastic sheets were tested and found to have a weight and strength similar to the metal. French bauxite (aluminium ore) deposits had fallen into the hands of the Germans, but Britain imported from other countries enough bauxite and aluminium for necessary

Supermarine Spitfire Mk 1 of No 609 Squadron in June 1940 *Engine:* **Rolls-Royce Merlin III, 1030 hp** *Armament:* **Eight .303-inch Browning machine guns** *Maximum speed:* **362 mph at 18,500 feet** *Initial climb rate:* **2,530 feet per minute** *Ceiling:* **31,900 feet** *Range:* **575 miles** *Weight loaded:* **6,200 lbs** *Wing loading:* **26 lbs per square foot** *Span:* **32 feet 10 inches** *Length:* **29 feet 11 inches**

war production – and most British housewives were willing to sacrifice their aluminium saucepans to the war effort – without having to change production methods radically for the manufacture of plastic aircraft.

By the end of March 1939, squadrons at Hornchurch fighter station were being equipped with Spitfires, and by April an Auxiliary Air Force (equivalent to the United States Air National Guard) squadron, No 602 City of Glasgow, received its first new fighter. When war broke out, 400 Spitfires were in service and the original order for 310 had been increased to over 2,000; the demand was so great that the works at Woolston had to be expanded and a shadow factory was built at Castle Bromwich, Birmingham. This latter factory was a government project and in 1938 Lord Nuffield, the Morris car manufacturer, was invited to run it. Another aircraft manufacturer, Westland, also prepared to make Spitfires and fifty Mk Is were made by that company. Progress at Castle Bromwich was very slow and when Lord Beaverbrook took over the new Ministry of Aircraft Production in May, 1940, none of the 1,500 Spitfires ordered had come off the assembly lines. Fortunately, Merlin production fared better and the vital engine – it was the only engine suitable for Britain's front line fighters – was in production at a new works at Crewe by May 1939. Another Merlin works opened near Glasgow in October, 1940 and the following year the Ford Company's Manchester plant began to manufacture Merlins. The period of

grace, negotiated by Chamberlain before Hitler sent his armies against Poland, was sufficient to get some squadrons equipped and experienced with Spitfires, for a few radar stations to become operative and for Fighter Command to test its communication networks.

Preparing for the coming air battles, Spitfire pilots trained at air-to-air gunnery (with camera gun or shooting at a towed drogue), dogfighting, formation flying and formation attacks. Experienced pilots who had flown other fighters – Gladiators, Defiants, Blenheims, Hurricanes – usually retrained in their squadrons after re-equipping with Spitfires, while pilots from advanced training depots spent a few weeks at an Operational Training Unit (OTU) before being posted to a fighter squadron. It soon became surprisingly obvious that pilots used to fixed undercarriage aircraft needed the reminder horn which blew when the throttle was cut back while the undercarriage was still in the 'up' position. The first two squadrons equipped with Spitfires, No 19 and No 66, were used to the fixed-undercarriage Gloster Gladiators and several pilots suffered the indignity of their new aircraft skidding across the field in an unintentional belly-landing, airscrews splintering as they wondered why the horn kept blowing.

In making diving attacks, pilots found the ailerons heavy at high speed and were restricted to a limit of 450 mph. Aerobatics were practised, not that they were essential for actual combat but they gave the pilot experience in the precise control over his aircraft necessary for the confidence to make an attack from any angle and extricate himself from enemy fighter attack. Hopefully, and for the mild thrill, trainee pilots also practised victory rolls – slow rolls low across the airfield – but some commanders banned them, for should an aircraft be damaged in the victorious battle it could be so weakened that a slow roll could cause it to crash – for such accidents had happened before.

On 11th October 1939, the formation of the Empire Air Training Scheme was announced in London. This scheme was to provide, every year, 50,000 volunteer aircrew from Britain, Canada, New Zealand, Rhodesia and South Africa, most of them trained or partly trained in their homelands.

An important adjunct to flying training was the development of the Link Trainer, an indoor cockpit of ingenious design which simulated the attitudes of flight – except for aerobatics. It could be 'stalled', collapsing in a nose-down position and revolving or 'spinning' on its pedestal. In a Link, which was worked by electrically driven pumps and gyroscopes, it was possible to practise navigation and exact flying on instruments. The hood of the Link was not transparent and the instructor sat at a desk from which he gave courses and heights to fly. The pilot's attempts to obey the instructions he received were recorded on a graph from which an assessment of his ability and progress could be made.

Night flying in a Spitfire was very difficult because the blue flames and sparks emitted from the engine through the exhausts were likely to dazzle the pilot, a thing which did not happen in daylight but which was of paramount importance at night. Although Spitfires rarely flew at night they often flew through cloud where the leader flew on instruments and the rest of the flight flew in close visual contact; if this contact were broken, formating pilots not only had fly carefully on instruments; but also

A pupil steps into a Link Trainer – the 'horror box' – while his instructor waits to put him through his paces on navigation and instrument flying

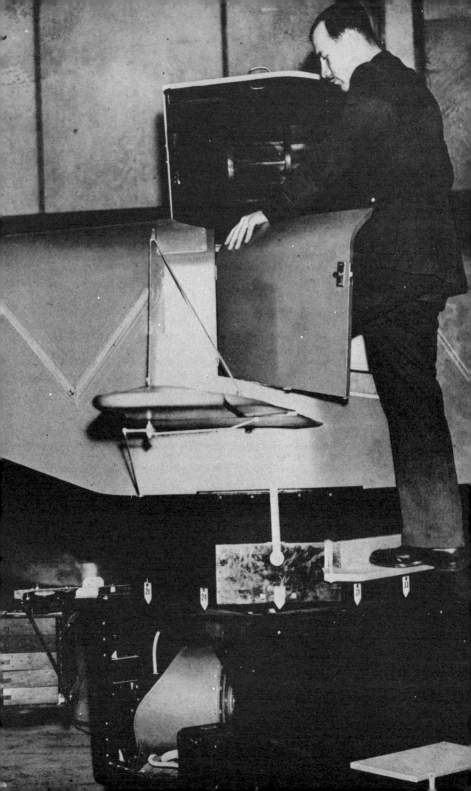

found it necessary to keep a lookout to avoid collision. Squadron and Wing formation flying through cloud slowed the climb to interception height and the hours spent on the Link helped to speed the operation and make sure everyone was capable of getting through; they called it the 'horror box'.

On some fighter and training stations twelve-bore shotguns and clays were supplied for fighter pilots to develop a feeling for deflection shooting – swinging easily along the flight of a clay and ahead of it to fire and score a hit helped to produce the idea of 'leading' (shooting ahead of) an enemy bomber or fighter when firing at an angle. Good shots with a twelve-bore were often good shots with eight machine guns when they filled their sights with a Messerschmitt or a Zero.

First shooting lessons with machine guns in the air were given by instructors in the two-seater trainers but all of the instruction with camera guns or real bullets did not help much in deflection shooting unless a pilot had some natural talent. In 1943, Link Trainers were equipped with simulated armament which was probably the best method of instruction and practice at OTUs in the absence of a super, wide-angle-lens camera or costly remote-controlled drones. Training at an OTU varied from a month to eight weeks but after Dunkirk some pilots had only a few days' instruction before they went on to their squadrons where, if there was time, they would be given further instruction by men who had been in action. In 1940, most pilots had to learn for themselves.

To help prevent 'night blindness' – temporary lessening of ability to see in the dark – instruments were illuminated with lamps which gave off a red glow, a colour which does not detract from night vision. The Spitfire's port and starboard lights were set unobtrusively in the wings just forward of the tips, the tail navigation light below the trimming tab on the rudder and upward identification lamp on the fuselage behind the radio mast. At elementary training schools all pilots learned to land without lights, judging with practice the relative positions of the marker beacons along the flarepath during approach and touchdown. This exercise was particularly beneficial to Spitfire pilots landing their aircraft with the long nose blanking out forward vision in the three-point attitude. It was safer to 'wheel it on' – land faster with the tail up and the landing path clearly visible, until the aircraft slowed down and the nose rose as the tail dropped and the straight-ahead view was hidden. The main landing lights were situated under the wings where they retracted pneumatically when not in use. As well as the bright exhaust dazzle, which was later reduced by baffles on the exhausts, the reflector sight could be slightly dazzling if turned up too bright at night.

The reflector sight (shown, for some extraordinary reason, to visiting Luftwaffe generals in 1937) was another piece of ingenuity incorporated into the armament of the Spitfire and most other British fighters. Replacing the old ring-and-bead sights, the reflector sight was a system of lenses which shone the image of a gun sight on to a small glass just behind the windshield inside the cockpit, the image intensity being adjustable for varying combat conditions. Thrown up by a lamp was a faint red circle with a dot in the centre. Running across the circle were two horizontal lines which could be adjusted inwards or outwards by turning a milled ring, graduated to represent the wingspans of various types of aircraft: when the enemy's wings filled the gap between the two lines it was within range. Deflection shooting, from above, below or from side-on, was a matter of judgement, but from head-on or astern the reflector sight did away with any uncertainty about distance. The intensity of the light of the reflector sight, and of the instruments, could be varied by turning the knob of the dimming switches. If the enemy were near enough it was possible to shoot accurately by guesswork should, for example, the reflector sight lamp blow in the middle of a dogfight. This happened to 'Paddy' Finucane while he was leading No 452 Squadron back across the French coast and into a swarm of Messerschmitts in August 1941. In his combat report he wrote:

'... I gave a three-second burst to the

rear one – a Messerschmitt 109F – from about seventy-five yards on a quarter attack. The enemy aircraft went down with smoke and flames coming from it . . . The bulb in my sight went unserviceable and while I was changing it, I was hopped by two Me 109s. Tainton warned me and I attacked the rear one without any sight. I did a full beam attack from ten yards range and blew his tail unit clean off.'

It wasn't necessary to get that close without the aid of a glowing sight. In this short and hectic battle the squadron shot down seven Me 109s. No Spitfires were lost.

The other requirement for good shooting was steadiness in the aircraft which was, after all, simply a gun carriage and platform and if it were to slip or skid during fighting, despite the reflector sight being 'on', the shots would go astray. The Hurricane was regarded as a steadier gun platform than the more sensitive Spitfire, yet judging by the results, the 'natural' shots seemed to do just as well in either aircraft. To check on the steadiness and to correct any slipping or skidding, pilots were taught to quickly refer to the 'turn and bank' indicator. This instrument is found in all aircraft and is a simple mechanism, a needle or ball that moves as a result of sideways thrust (moving left or right of the centre line if there is any slipping during a turn, or skidding in a dive or in level flight). Unlike gyroscopic instruments, which tumble during violent manoeuvres and are temporarily useless after them, the turn and bank indicator functions throughout the spectrum of aerobatics.

In the Spitfire IA there was one firing button on the circular handle of the control column; in Spitfires with cannon the round button was replaced by a rectangular button which fired both cannon and machine guns when pressed in the centre, machine guns only when pressed at the top and cannon only when the bottom part of the button was pressed. The camera-gun, originally installed for training purposes and later an essential recorder of 'kills' for official confirmation was also activated by the trigger button. In training flights a separate button on the stick handle was used for shooting with the camera gun which was set in the port wing root and aimed parallel to the guns. Cloth patches were glued over the eight gun-ports in the wings and the patches were blown off with the first burst, which was usually fired to test the guns before going into action.

Maximum range for the 0.303 inch Brownings was 1,000 yards but at that distance the bullets would have scattered over a wide area, as the guns were usually aimed so that five of the guns met (in an 'apex of convergance') 250 yards in front of the nose. Originally the guns were aimed to form a large, spread-out bullet pattern so that the average pilot would have a chance of making some strikes on the enemy, an aiming system eventually proved to be a waste of hitting power. Eventually all guns were altered to a narrow cone of fire, sending out a stream of bullets which converged then spread again to a width of a few yards within a distance of 500 yards. In the few seconds available in which to destroy or cripple an enemy aircraft, the concentration of eight guns firing a total of 8,000 rounds per minute was frequently enough to knock a fatal hole in the wings, fuselage or tail if they missed the vital cockpit or engine. Four machine guns and two cannon were more lethal still – 4,000 bullets and 1,200 shells per minute – a total weight of fire of 410 pounds per minute leaving the guns.

One of the pioneers of military flying during the First World War was the commander of the Royal Flying Corps, Brigadier-General H M Trenchard, 'Father' of the Royal Air Force; as its Chief of the Air Staff he was Air-Chief-Marshal Sir Hugh Trenchard and later Marshal of the Royal Air Force. Viscount Trenchard, known as 'Boom' for his loud-hailer voice, moulded the RAF into what it was when war broke out in 1939. He aimed at giving his aircrews as much training as possible but the neat, tight and accurate formations devised were the wrong kind for fighting – in either war. The new pilots in their Mk Is flew in 'vic' (V-shaped) formations of three to a section, four sections to a squadron. They were taught to form into a line-astern

pattern for section attacks and sections to come in one after the other to make their attacks. It was like a parade ground drill and the different types of attack were numbered resulting in this sort of order: 'B Flight, form up for a No 1 attack . . . Go!' It took the severe learning of lessons inflicted by the Germans on the British during the Battle of Britain to untie the red tape tactics and make the RAF painfully relearn the successful methods evolved by fighter or 'scout' pilots on both sides in the First World War, from Boelcke to Mannock, to fly in loose but vigilant formations consisting of small but very closely integrated teams of small numbers of aircraft. These lessons were once again learnt by the Luftwaffe in the Spanish Civil War.

Spitfire pilots were in touch with each other and ground stations through their High Frequency (HF), later Very High Frequency (VHF), transmitter-receivers set well back in the middle of the fuselage and reached through a side panel for maintenance. The aerial led through the fuselage to the top of the short aerial mast behind the cockpit to the tip of the rudder above its hinges. Identification Friend or Foe (IFF) – an automatic device to indicate British aircraft to ground stations – had aerials on early model Spitfires running from the fuselage to the tips of the tailplane. The pilot wore a rubber oxygen face-mask moulded to cover nose, mouth and chin, clipped on to the helmet, the microphone built into the mask and the earphones attached to the leather flying helmet. Microphone and the earphones were connected to a single universal plug which was pushed into the radio socket, which had four channels, marked from A to D. In areas where radio silence was imperative, radios were switched on for reception only and flight leaders used hand signals where necessary although the 'follow the leader' system did away with most of the need for hand signals. The twelve-volt accumulator battery was attached to the bottom of the fuselage, in front of the radio and behind the pilot. Above the battery was the oxygen bottle, easily accessible through a fuselage panel. A tube led

Viscount Trenchard, the 'father' of the Royal Air Force

the oxygen to the cockpit where there was an attachment for the pilot's face-mask tube. A gauge showed the amount of flow from bottle to mask.

On the other side of the pilot's padded head-rest fixed to the armour plate was the voltage regulator box, underneath which were two long bottles of compressed air which provided power for brakes, flaps, and undercarriage landing lights and triggered the guns. The pneumatic brakes were connected to the rudder pedals which operated the amount of braking on each wheel after the air had been allowed to go through to the brakes by moving the handle on the control column. This system saved weight and gave pilots with injured legs, and the few pilots with artificial legs, control when taxiing, impossible in aircraft where the brakes were applied by depressing an upper bar on the rudder pedal. The Spitfire's pneumatic system was very powerful, providing quick and positive flap and undercarriage movement.

At first sight the cockpit seemed to be laid out in a very confused order but after a few hours' familiarisation pilots found the instruments easy to read and conveniently grouped, and the levers, switches and buttons placed in handy positions, a vital point because in a 'scramble' – quick start and take-off – it was necessary to manipulate the various levers, switches and buttons without looking. The cockpit was unlined and the light metal bucket seat unpadded. Below the gunsight switches was the dashboard with the main flying instruments – airspeed indicator, altimeter, artificial horizon (showing the aircraft's lateral and longitudinal attitudes in relation to the horizontal and vertical planes), direction indicator (an 'artificial compass' showing heading readings), rate of climb indicator (graduated in hundreds of feet per minute) and turn-and-bank indicator. To the right of this rubber-mounted panel was another group of instruments: engine-revolution counter, oil and fuel pressure gauges, engine boost gauge, oil and radiator temperature gauges and fuel gauges; below was the fuel cock. At the top left-hand side of the panel were the flap lever and flap position indicator; below these were the undercarriage indicator, flying position indicator, air pressure control, light switch and landing light lever. Rheostat light switches for the instruments were fitted below the instrument panel.

On the right of the cockpit were the undercarriage selector lever and undercarriage emergency hand pump, and the key for recognition-light signalling; on the left were the radio switch and channel selection buttons, throttle and pitch control levers, trimming-tab knobs and levers for controlling radiator flap and seat positions. For parking, the brakes were locked on and two rods brought into the cockpit to hold the control column firmly in an upright position.

There were no trimming tabs for the ailerons as there were for the fabric-covered elevators and rudder. The skid of the prototype was replaced by a swivelling tail-wheel on the Mk I. On all production marks up to the Mk VII the tail-wheel was of the non-retractable type. A rear-view mirror was fitted on top of the windscreen in order that the pilot might spot any enemy aircraft trying to close up on his tail unseen.

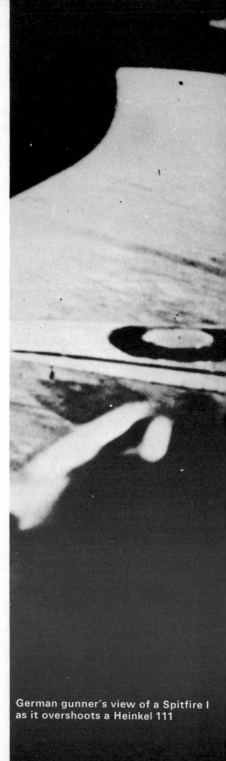

German gunner's view of a Spitfire I as it overshoots a Heinkel 111

The Battle of Britain

There were many small modifications which could be made to improve the Spitfire, and while the Mk II was being prepared the Mk I went to war. Before 'Eagle Day', Göring's *Adler Tag*, which would inaugurate the Luftwaffe operation to endeavour to destroy the RAF, Spitfires had already seen action. The first contact was made on 16th October over the Firth of Forth where Heinkel He 111 bombers narrowly missed hitting British warships anchored a few hundred yards east of the old Forth bridge. No 603 Squadron, whose pilots were mostly young Scotsmen of the Auxiliary Air Force, was based at Turnhouse airfield, and when the Luftwaffe sent a reconnaissance aircraft high over the Firth and Rosyth naval base, No 602 and No 603 Squadrons, both equipped with Spitfires, were alerted to expect a bombing attack to follow the reconnaissance, and Fighter Command ordered the squadrons to patrol the naval base area. The bombers duly flew on the expected mission and Red Section of No 603 made contact with the enemy. The leader of this section was the squadron commander, Squadron-Leader E E Stevens, who ordered the section into line astern for an attack in regulation style, dived to fire first then broke away as his Number Two and Number Three followed to make their attacks: a bomber was shot down into the sea and Stevens was awarded the 'kill'. Another pilot damaged a second German bomber and three more were dispersed then chased into cloud cover.

Again over Scotland, on 28th October, a Spitfire shot an He 111 down into the heather on the Lammermuir Hills, the first enemy aircraft to be brought down on British soil in the Second World War – and the first since 1918. A Heinkel bomber was another 'first' to Spitfires – the first enemy aircraft to be brought down over England, on 20th November. So far the score was three to none but the Spitfire had not encountered any Me 109 fighters or Me 110 two-seater fighter-bombers that the Luftwaffe called *Zerstörer* (Destroyer).

Parade-ground precision as a vic of Spitfire Is banks round in the way favoured by the RAF in early 1940

Bombers – the Spitfire's most
important prey during the
Battle of Britain. Here a Heinkel 111
(at bottom) receives a burst of
machine gun fire. Its port engine is
already on fire

In the early part of 1940, Göring directed his bombers against shipping in the Channel and coastal ports, hindering raids that tested defences, while his main air forces were withheld, during the 'phoney war' period, in readiness for the strong blows yet to be made across the Low Countries. The Spitfire squadrons were restricted to Home Defence while several Hurricane squadrons had gone to France in the Advanced Air Striking Force supporting the British Expeditionary Force (BEF). The Hurricane pilots saw a lot of action after the Blitzkrieg had been set in motion once again on 10th May 1940, and by the time the BEF had been squeezed back on the beaches of Dunkirk, nearly 300 fighter pilots had been lost in action against every type of fighter and bomber the Germans possessed. The surviving pilots brought back vital information on the enemy's fighting tactics and were able to instruct from actual experience. After returning to Britain, many of these pilots joined squadrons re-equipping with Spitfires.

The first full-scale clash between Spitfires and Me 109s occurred on 23rd May 1940. A squadron commander marooned at Calais was considered important enough to be picked up by air courier – a two-seater Miles Master trainer – escorted by two Spitfire Is. During this operation the three RAF aircraft were attacked by twelve Me 109s, three of which were destroyed and two damaged. The Spitfires, the Miles Master and the rescued commander all returned safely to England. Spitfires were victors in the first clash between the world's two best fighters, winning against superior numbers; this was to be the pattern of the future battle looming in the summer of 1940.

When the awesome success of German arms forced the BEF back to the French coast, Dowding released the Spitfire squadrons from their restricted close Channel flights to assist in covering the withdrawal of the British troops. Hitler believed that the canals, dykes and flooded country around Dunkirk might bog down his valuable Panzers, all of which could then be destroyed in a last-ditch battle with the British artillery. There was still a large French army

to be defeated so Hitler left the destruction of the evacuating British troops to four *Fliegerkorps* of Göring's Luftwaffe.

Bad weather from 28th/30th May handicapped operations for both air forces but the next day was clear and air battles raged over the beaches where 68,000 troops were taken off in all kinds of craft. German guns close to the shore were inflicting more damage than the Luftwaffe, but at night the scene was illuminated with parachute flares for the German bombers, practically immune from the inadequate RAF night fighters, to choose their targets. The bombers could fly in from the clouds, drop their bombs and disappear back into cloud, leaving the unfortunate men on shore or in sinking ships with the impression that the RAF was missing. Yet nearly the entire fighter force of RAF, except for three of its squadrons protecting the naval bases in Scotland, were in action over the Channel or the Dunkirk area during the evacuation which lasted from 21st May to 4th June, and during this period many air battles were fought between sea level and 30,000 feet. Over 338,000 soldiers were carried away from Dunkirk but six British destroyers were among the 243 craft sunk and the RAF lost over eighty pilots and 229 fighters.

The air fighting over Dunkirk was desperate as the British pilots concentrated on the bombers, time and again leaving themselves vulnerable to attacks by enemy fighters. Naturally some squadrons were in action more than others and some fighter pilots flew until they were exhausted: one fell into such a sound sleep after landing from his last flight of the day that he had to be lifted out of the cockpit. Altogether the pilots claimed 377 German fighters and bombers but the Germans later claimed that they lost only about 140, including a number to fire from warships.

After 4th June, for a few short weeks, Fighter Command was able to rest its pilots and prepare its interceptors for the defence of the homeland, short of sixty-seven Spitfires and 386 Hurricanes lost so far in air fighting. Without knowing very much about the Me 109, Spitfire pilots had come to believe that the enemy machine might be about equal in performance to their aircraft and that in an equal-number contest it would be flying, shooting ability and aggressiveness that would tip the balance in favour of the eventual victors. No matter which aircraft was better, it could be shot down by the other if its pilot was in a position, through good flying or luck, to fire – and the only limiting factors would be that his aim would have to be accurate and his plane steady when the firing-button was pressed.

In the fighting over Dunkirk, one fault, not considered serious before, handicapped Spitfires in combat: when the stick was pushed forward suddenly the motor momentarily spluttered as a result of having its fuel supply cut off in the carburettor which was of the normal float type. This slight hesitation in flight was an advantage to an Me 109 both in attack and in evasion since it did not falter in dives. Fortunately a couple of Me 109s had been captured intact during the fighting in France, and one was brought back to England. During evaluation tests against a Spitfire, at the Royal Aircraft Establishment at Farnborough, the most important difference between the two aircraft was found to be that when negative 'G' was applied, by pushing the stick forward roughly, the Daimler-Benz engine did not splutter because of its direct fuel-injection system. The Spitfire was proved to be more manoevrable, both had similar speeds in dives, the Me 109 climbing slightly faster and at some heights was faster in straight and level flight, and was better equipped for assisting the pilot to resist 'G' forces because he sat with his knees bent higher, giving him higher resistance against blackouts. As a result of the Me 109 test an extension was added to the Spitfire rudder pedals and the two-position helped to counteract 'G' forces as well as providing a little extra comfort on long flights. The VDM three-blade constant-speed airscrew was the factor that gave the Me 109 its advantage in climbing. In Britain it had already been decided to equip fighters with a constant-speed unit and de Havilland were asked to rush conversion kits to squadrons and instruct mechanics in

how to carry out the change. Previously, all production of constant-speed airscrews had gone to the bombers which required every assistance to get their large loads off the ground. As well as airscrews there were engine pipes and quill shafts to be produced for the conversions, but the process of converting Spitfires to the new airscrew units took place in a remarkably short time. Sometimes these hydraulically operated units developed leaks in the lines and oil flowed back along the cowling, creeping on to the windscreen. To clear it off during flight was rather difficult, the pilot having to slow the plane to about 85 mph to wipe the windscreen with his hand pressed closely around it to prevent his arm being whipped back in the slipstream.

In 1936 the Air Council split RAF flying administration into Bomber, Fighter, Coastal and Training Commands, and in 1938 formed Maintenance, Balloon and Reserve Commands. Fighter Command Headquarters were established at Bentley Priory, a mansion built in 1770 at Stanmore, an outer north-west London suburb. Beneath the stately oldworld appearance of Bentley Priory and its grounds there was eventually built a modern underground structure containing the Operations and Filter Rooms, buried deep and strengthened with reinforced concrete, called 'The Hole', connected with fighter, radar, army anti-aircraft, Observer Corps and Balloon Command stations throughout Britain. From 1939, the heads of Fighter Command, Air-Marshal Dowding and his successors, controlled these five service arms and the air-raid warning systems, and planned the strategies of defence and attack.

Tactical planning was done in the subordinate Groups, commanded by Air-Commodores or Air Vice-Marshals (equivalent to USAAF Brigadier-Generals and Major-Generals), and each Group was made up of several stations under the control of a Wing-Commander or Group-Captain (equivalent to Lieutenant-Colonel or Colonel). On each station were one or more squadrons, each led by a Squadron-Leader (equivalent to a Major). The station commanders were pilots,

most of them with combat experience
gained on the Western Front in the
First World War, as indeed had the
more senior commanders of Fighter
Command and the Groups. Commanders of stations (certain fighter
bases were known as 'sector stations')
and commanders of Groups were men
whose leadership was active; they
were not expected or supposed to fly
in the formations, for there could not
be two commanders in the air, but
they often went up in Hurricanes or
Spitfires to have a look at what went
on, sometimes finding a place in a
formation or more often flying alone.
Air Vice-Marshal Keith Park, who
held the lonely and responsible command of the forward 11 Group, often
flew his Hurricane to observe the
fighting.

Group-Captain Victor Beamish, the
Irish commander of North Weald
sector station, often flew alone to an
interception area to see for himself
how the fighting progressed, alert for
any stray enemy aircraft to line up in
his sights. He was flying together with
the commander of his station's wing,
Wing-Commander Boyd, on an intruder flight across the Channel, when
they spotted the *Scharnhorst*, *Gneisenau* and *Prinz Eugen* leaving Brest on
their way up the Channel on 12th
February 1942. Both were lucky not to
have had their Spitfires shot down by
the huge fighter swarms covering the
German warships. Air fighting in fast
machines was a young man's game
and anyone over thirty-six – with
some exceptions – was handicapped
with slightly lowered judgement and
co-ordination and, most important,
lessened ability to sight the enemy at
long distance. Beamish was eventually jumped and shot down on one of
his lone flights. Station commanders
could be a distraction to squadron
leaders who felt that they had to keep
an eye on them, but they were persis-
tent. One of the Atcherley twins –
both were excellent pilots, Group-
Captains in 1940 – was shot down in his
Spitfire the day after the C-in-C Fighter
Command had ordered him to stay
out of the fighting. The twins survived the war and both attained air
rank (equivalent to general rank).

The commander of Northolt sector
station was Group-Captain Vincent

Group-Captain Victor Beamish was one of several station commanders who used Spitfires for individual reconnaissance flights

who maintained a Hurricane for his own use and 'station defence'. Vincent scrambled off in his plane one day when there were no fighters in the vicinity of a raid approaching the station. He intercepted the German formation of about forty Dornier bombers and Me 109 fighters, diving into the middle of them and shooting down an Me 109. He saw another Me 109 shot down by one of its own companions in the confusion resulting from his wild attack.

The RAF higher command had a strong common bond with their junior commanders and pilots. Although permanent and long-term members of the RAF, and therefore liable to develop inflexible attitudes, the senior men, by virtue of the fact that they had been fighter and bomber pilots themselves, could understand and be receptive to suggestions from the new

generation. Air Vice-Marshals were understanding if squadron and wing commanders did not pay heed to the great cloud of officious bureaucratic petty regulations and correspondence that showered down from the senior chair-borne officers more interested in administration than fighting.

When France fell, the main strength of Britain's fighter forces was concentrated in the south-east of England, from Cambridge and Martlesham Heath in the north, down around the coast and inland to Middle Wallop in Hampshire and Warmwell in Dorset. Around London itself were the airfields of Kenley, Biggin Hill, Debden, Hornchurch and Northolt, with more easterly fields at Gravesend, Eastchurch, Manston and Hawkinge. Around Southampton were Warmwell, Middle Wallop, Westhampshire, Tangmere and the Fleet Air Arm station at Gosport. Seven sector stations and a few satellite airfields (smaller and less well prepared landing strips with only minor maintenance and living facilities, attached to the sector

stations for use if the main station was put out of service) were under the control of 11 Group, which had its headquarters at Uxbridge, the station where T E Lawrence once sought anonymity as an aircraftsman. The commander of this group was a New Zealander, Air-Vice-Marshal Keith Park, whose squadrons formed the front line of defence and were to take the brunt of the fighting in the coming battle. There were fourteen Hurricane, six Spitfire and two Blenheim squadrons in Park's 11 Group and he could call on support from his neighbouring groups, 10 Group in the west and 12 Group in the north.

10 Group was commanded by Air-Vice-Marshal Sir Quitin Brand whose Headquarters were at Box, in Wiltshire; 12 Group was commanded by Air-Vice-Marshal Trafford Leigh-Mallory at Watnall, in Nottinghamshire; and defending northern England and Scotland was 13 Group, commanded by Air-Vice-Marshal R E Saul at Newcastle upon Tyne. The fighter stations in these groups were Church Fenton, Kirton-in-Lindsey, Digby, Coltishall and Wittering in 12 Group; Pembrey, Filton, St Eval and Middle Wallop in 10 Group; and Catterick, Usworth, Wick, Dyce and Turnhouse in 13 Group. Their squadrons numbered thirty-seven, of which fourteen flew Spitfires, seventeen Hurricanes, four Blenheims and two Defiants. There was also a flight of Air Fleet Arm Gladiators. Including the squadrons that were forming and re-equipping with Spitfires and Hurricanes, the RAF had under 700 single-engined fighters.

The Luftwaffe assembled by the end of July 800 Me 109s and 240 Me 110 fighters, 1,100 bombers and 300 Ju 87 dive-bombers in *Luftflotten* Two and Four based in Holland, Belgium and northern France, and another 100 fighters and 120 bombers of *Luftflotte* Five based in Norway and Denmark. *Luftflotte* Two, operating from Holland and Belgium, was commanded by

Field-Marshal Albert Kesselring in Brussels, *Luftflotte* Three from northern France by Field-Marshal Hugo Sperrle in Paris and *Luftflotte* Five from Denmark and Norway by General Hans-Jorgen Stumpff in Kristiansand. Two of Germanys' most able unit commanders, Major Adolf Galland and Major Werner Mölders, led squadrons based in France.

German Intelligence had made a thorough study of RAF fighter dispositions and defences but was very wide of the mark concerning the quality of its aircraft and pilots: Göring was led to believe that the Spitfire was inferior to the Me 109 and was not much better than the Me 110. He announced that it would take the Luftwaffe only a few days, not weeks, to destroy the Spitfires and all the other British fighters and bombers. To discover what the British had in the way of radio defence, elaborate tests had been made in 1939 by flying an airship equipped as a laboratory along the English Channel coast. The German scientists suspected that there was some sort of warning system, but specific details were not obtained, though Göring was advised that the tall masts and little buildings at Swingate, Rye, Pevensey and Ventnor, on the Isle of Wight, could be valuable warning devices. Robert Watson-Watt's radar was much more important than Göring considered it to be and his negligence in not ordering continuous and heavier attacks on these and other radar stations was one of the many strategic blunders made by the Germans during the battle. Experiments with radio-location equipment had also been made by the Germans but their techniques, though fairly advanced by 1940, were not thought important by the High Command. Without radar, Britain could easily have lost the battle – and the war. Other important radio investigations in Britain were successful in countering German radio navigation aids used for guiding bombers on to English cities.

The first skirmishes began in the long daylight hours of July with German bombers and dive-bombers, escorted by fighters, attacking ships in the Straits of Dover and testing the fighter defences. Two Spitfires were

Nerve centre of the fighter defences during the Battle – the Operations Room of Fighter Command, under Bentley Priory in Middlesex

shot down, the pilots baling out, when they were jumped by Me 109s while making an attack on a group of Me 110s, the first of many occasions when the Spitfires would be meeting the Me 109s in similar circumstances – Me 109s attacking from above while the Spitfires were busy with bombers or Me 110s or other Me 109s. The Germans had remembered the lessons of from the First World War, flying in pairs (a *rotte*) or in two pairs, in the position of the four finger tips (a *schwarms*) keeping high with the sun behind them. The RAF was beginning to learn again to 'beware of the Hun in the sun'.

In the small skirmishes there was usually hard fighting for Spitfire and Hurricane pilots, mostly outnumbered and forced into a dual role of having first to protect the shipping by attacking the bombers and then to defend themselves from the accompanying German fighters. Many of the engagements were fleeting, and the attacks were made often, over a wide area and on many small ships. Sometimes the British fighters flew up to 600 sorties a day but could not always be on the spot when a ship was attacked. Sometimes no one was shot down on either side but usually the Germans lost at a rate of more than two to one. An outstanding exception was when nine Boulton-Paul Defiants, single-engined two-seater fighters with a power-operated four-gun turret as their only armament, were attacked by twenty Me 109s: six Defiants were shot down while all but one of the Me 109s escaped the fire of the British gunners. The Spitfire and Hurricane pilots were picking up valuable experience in the fights around Dover's 'Hellfire Corner'. Dowding had no worries about fuel with stocks increasing every week; he was, however, concerned with the narrow margin of reserves for aircraft (only at the beginning of the battle) and pilot replacements (throughout the battle).

Because not one Spitfire had come out of the new Castle Bromwich factory by May, Lord Beaverbrook ordered Vickers to take it over. By the end of June only ten new Spitfires Mark IIs with the more powerful Merlin XII, had been delivered; by the end of September another 115 were flying. The Battle of Britain Spitfires

were Mk Is, except for a few Mk IIs.

While the preliminary skirmishes were developing, Hitler was beginning to feel the effects of victory and realising how powerful his armies were. Italy had entered the war on 10th June and Marshal Pétain had asked for armistice terms on 17th June; almost two million Frenchmen had been taken prisoner and at Oran and Mersel-Kébir the Royal Navy was forced to make a neutralising attack on former Allied French capital ships. The outlook for Britain was anything but hopeful and Hitler was confident that his public peace appeal, his 'final appeal to common sense', made in a Reichstag address on 19th July, would end the conflict. This was the day that Britain lost eight aircraft, including the six Defiants. When Lord Halifax, the British Foreign Secretary, rejected Hitler's offer on 22nd July, Hitler went ahead with plans drawn up for the operation he code-named '*Seelöwe*' (Sea Lion), the invasion of England: he issued orders for the Luftwaffe 'to overcome the British air force with all means at its disposal, and as soon as possible'.

The first large-scale raid on Britain was made on 10th July, which some historians reckon to be the date for the beginning of the battle; official histories, however, make 12th August the day of the beginning, the day the Luftwaffe attacked radar stations and coastal airfields. As far as the RAF were concerned they had been in plenty of fights since 10th July and on 8th August the RAF had lost nineteen fighters while shooting down thirty-one German aircraft. Both sides had claimed higher numbers downed, honest miscalculations in most cases; actual figures for the results of big dogfighting actions could not be assessed accurately until after the war and then there remained some confusion as a result of lost or destroyed records and a few deliberate alterations by the Germans.

On this day, Air Vice-Marshal Park was suddenly confronted with his battle when Stukas attacked convoys

Right top and bottom: **Familiar sights in the skies of 1940 – hordes of German bombers and skeins of vapour trails**

in the Thames estuary, Portsmouth was bombed, feints were made along the coasts, radar stations at Dover, Rye, Pevensey and Ventnor were bombed as well as the airfields at Lympne, Manston and Hawkinge. That night, several cities, towns and villages were attacked in small raids which Göring hoped would inspire panic in the population. Manston airfield was a prime target and on this first day it was defended by Spitfires from No 54 Squadron which could not get at the bombers for the Me 109s. No 65 Squadron's Spitfires were taking off when the bombs came tumbling down and only one Spitfire got off before the field was pitted with craters. One radar station was in fact knocked out for some time, but the Germans could perhaps be forgiven for thinking that they had ruined others for their bombs caused a lot of damage. They had not, however, destroyed the morale of the first Women's Auxiliary Air Force (WAAF) girls to

Below: Blenheims should have been used as intruders *Right:* Heinkel IIIs storm in over the south coast

come under fire, for these stayed at their posts at the radar stations and at vector station Operations Rooms during the weeks that the battle lasted.

The Germans also believed that Manston was out of the war and that No 65 Squadron was written off. The truth was that the RAF lost twenty-two aircraft altogether during the 730 sorties flown during that day and from bombing on three airfields. The Germans lost thirty-one. As the battle progressed Park had to learn how best to deal with superior numbers flying in at different altitudes from different directions to different targets. His primitive radar could inform him when the enemy was building up its bomber and fighter formations over the French coast, but as they approached, radar could not give him their height and he had to rely on information passed from visual sightings by Observer Corps posts signalled through Fighter Command to his Operations Room. Therefore, with so many points to defend, he felt that he must wait until the Luftwaffe's target was known before he could

direct his small groups of fighters to its defence. Had he met the Germans over the Channel with larger wing formations, and failed to intercept, the airfields and radar stations and other positions would be too vulnerable; he had no choice other than to try and break up every German attack and the only way he could possibly do this was to use small groups of fighters to intercept after the enemy's intentions were known.

13th August was Göring's 'Eagle Day' which began with a false start by the Luftwaffe when only a small part of its force attacked. Eastchurch airfield was bombed, the Operations Room being hit, five Blenheims destroyed and fifty craters formed on the field. Göring was deluded into believing that ten Spitfires were knocked out on the ground and that Eastchurch was out of action; it was, but only for one day. The German bombers were easily disconcerted when attacked and many dropped their bombs and fled, as happened when Spitfires intercepted Ju 88s heading for Odiham and Farnborough. Attacks increased in the afternoon, when the invaders were aided by cloud cover. Fires were started in warehouses and docks at Southampton by Ju 88s, and Spitfires from No 609 dived through the protecting Me 109s to shoot down nine Ju 87 Stukas on the way to bomb Middle Wallop. A No 609 pilot also got an Me 109. Detling fighter station was put out of action for one day, as its Operations Room was destroyed, the commanding officer killed and communications disrupted. Spitfires had intercepted but had been forced to deal with the bombers' escorting fighters; this engagement gave the bombers freedom of movement of the sort necessary to damage fighter airfields severely. The German force should have been overwhelming, over 1,400 sorties being flown, but they lost forty-five aircraft to the RAF's thirteen, and in claiming eighty-eight destroyed, the Germans were adding to their eventual confusion. That night the Spitfire shadow factory at Castle Bromwich was bombed, delaying production. The following day the RAF lost eight fighters and the Germans nineteen aircraft.

15th August was a decisive day when

An inquisitive guard pokes about in the wreckage of a Me-110 – the fighter which itself needed fighter protection in the Battle of Britain

heavy raids were mounted by the three *Luftflotten* against airfields and radar stations. In Scotland, the warning was early enough to get Spitfires and Hurricanes into position to intercept sixty-five bombers and thirty-four Me 110 fighters. No 72 Squadron's twelve Spitfires made contact, one section attacking the bombers, the other the fighters; the bombers were split up by the few Spitfires and the Me 110s huddled into a protective circle: the German fighter pilots' warning, '*Achtung Schpitfeuer*' had a frightening effect on Me 110s. Some of the bombers continued on to the coast where a group was intercepted by Spitfires of No 79 Squadron and another group by Hurricanes of No 605. Without loss, the RAF shot down eight bombers and seven fighters and damaged several other Luftwaffe planes. In an attack on Driffield in Yorkshire, ten obsolete Whitley bombers were destroyed on the ground, but *Luftflotte* Five lost another eight bombers to fighters from 12 Group. Hawkinge, Lympne, Manston, Martlesham Heath, Eastchurch and Middle Wallop were strafed or bombed or suffered both types of attack, and the radar stations at Dover, Rye, Foreness and Bawdsey were also bombed but not destroyed. The sun was still up at six pm when plots showed up again on the radar screens and although intercepted, bombers got through to bomb West Malling's runways and buildings. Then Croydon and two small factories on the outskirts of London were bombed and during the short hours of the summer darkness ten industrial towns, from Southampton to Birmingham, were bombed by small groups of raiders.

The Germans believed at the time that the RAF had suffered heavily, with airfields and radar stations put out of action and many aircraft destroyed. Actually the RAF had lost only thirty-four aircraft and seventeen pilots killed where the Luftwaffe had lost seventy-five aircraft (the original British claim was 182). The full German fighter force had achieved practically nothing in its attempt to destroy Fighter Command and the British fighter successes meant that in the future even the Me 110 'Destroyers' would need Me 109 protection.

Winston Churchill was at Fighter Command Headquarters that day, watching the plots moved by WAAFs using long rods across the charting table. The Prime Minister saw for himself the almost total commitment of the country's interceptor force against the hordes of enemy fighters and bombers. At the end of the day he was able to count the numbers of intact squadrons returning to their bases and watch the plots of enemy aircraft returning to France.

It was on this day, 15th August, that he was inspired to remark, 'Never in the field of human conflict was so much owed by so many to so few'.

On the next day, the Ventnor radar station was further damaged and Tangmere sector station suffered a heavy bombing which destroyed three Blenheims and damaged seven Hurricanes and four other aircraft. At Brize Norton, forty-six trainer aircraft were destroyed in blazing hangars of a flying training school. In the air, eight pilots were killed and twenty-two aircraft were shot down while the Germans lost forty-five. On 18th August the Germans lost another seventy-one aircraft and the RAF twenty-seven with ten pilots killed.

Throughout the battle, British pilots flew at a distinct advantage, because they were over their own country. This meant that if a pilot were shot down unwounded he could go straight back to his unit and return to the battle with the minimum of delay. Wounded pilots could be taken to hospital quickly, thereby reducing the chance of their having to spend a long time out of action. Beside this, the British aircraft shot down could be recovered and perhaps repaired or 'cannibalised' for other spare parts, whereas this was impossible for the Germans, as their aircraft fell on hostile soil. The same also applied to German pilots, who became POWs if they landed in Britain. They stood little chance unless they ditched in the Channel, where they might be picked up by German rescue services, or flew back to France in a perhaps seriously wounded condition.

The RAF pilots wore Mae West flotation jackets but did not carry

'Scramble'

Left: The squadron Intelligence officer listens to an account of the last battle and tries to assess how many aircraft have been shot down by these men individually and by the squadron as a whole. *Above:* While the pilots try to recoup their energies, armourers reload and repair the guns in time for the next sortie

Down in the drink! An airman waits
to be picked up by the Air-Sea
Rescue launch in the Channel

rubber dinghies in their parachute packs during the battle. This meant that some pilots, particularly those who may have been wounded or carried away by the currents, were drowned. Air-sea rescue was minimal at the outset of the battle until spotter aircraft and naval launches were brought in to help. They were respected by both sides, as they picked up all airmen found in the water. Supermarine Walrus float planes effected many rescues and sometimes floated on the Channel within sight of an enemy rescue float-plane also waiting to pick up downed airmen. A special SOS radio channel was kept open between Fighter Command and the Luftwaffe so that both could be advised of the whereabouts of pilots shot down near each other's coasts. Because of pilot losses over the 'drink', Park ordered his fighters to stay over land and not to chase every aircraft running for France.

Park also ordered patrols to be flown over the stations while raiders were being intercepted in case any sneak raiders got through. The bulk of the fighters were ordered to attack the bombers as it was these that caused the damage, and only a minimum number were to attack the escorting enemy fighters. If a sector aerodrome appeared to be the target for an attack, all aircraft from the station were to patrol above and just below the cloud base.

By 20th August, the first of the Polish squadrons had got their 'pilot's English' to a sufficient standard for reliable flying communication and they gleefully flew into action. It was not long before they began to establish a reputation for fearlessness and aggressiveness in diving among enemy bombers, with apparent disregard for their own safety.

The English vocabulary for air fighting was not very wide; the important communication was instruction on how and why the various tactics were to be applied. A good example of dog-fighting dialogue would contain little of the text-book 'No 1 attack Go!' and there was always a little confusion when too many pilots spoke or shouted warnings without identifying the actual Spitfire or Hurricane being attacked. Code names were used for

the vector station, where the controller was in touch with Fighter Command, for the squadron and for its leader; the enemy were usually called 'bandits' and the Germans usually called the RAF aircraft 'Red Indians'. In *Reach for the Sky*, Paul Brickhill's biography of Douglas Bader, the author recorded these quotes from an actual radio log of No 616 (Spitfire) Squadron:

'Fifty plus near two o'clock' (from the controller to Bader whose codename was Dogsbody).

'I haven't got 'em Johnny. What are they doing?'

'O.K., D.B. No immediate panic. They're going across us. I'm watching 'em.'

'O.K., O.K., I see 'em.'

(Silence for a while.) Then:

'Aircraft behind.'

'Aircraft three o'clock.'

'Aircraft below.' (Reports from various pilots.)

'Turning right Bus Company.' (Bader to his squadron.)

'109's overhead.'

'O.K. I see 'em.'

'Aircraft behind. Muck in, everybody.' (Bader.)

'Tell me when to break. I can't see the bastards.'

'Six bastards behind us.'

'I can see 'em in my mirror.'

'Two aircraft below.'

Then some Messerschmitts must have attacked.

'Break right.'

'He nearly had you, Cocky.' (Bader to Flying Officer Dundas.)

'Four right above.'

'Right on top of you.'

'Get organised.'

'I'm . . . . . if I can.'

'Four behind and above.'

'O.K. I'm looking after you.'

'Look behind.'

'It's only me. Don't get the wind up.'

'All right, you . . . !'

'Don't . . . about. We'll have some collisions in a minute.' (Apparently re-forming after an attack.)

'They're hell cat boys.' (Probably a Canadian.)

'Your R/T sounds bloody awful.'

Right: Douglas Bader poses beside a Hurricane of No 242 Squadron.

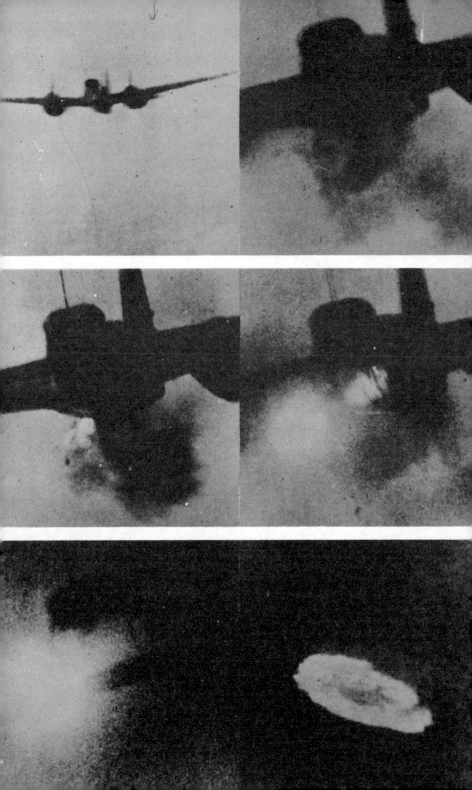

'Is mine O.K.?'

'Just like a lily.'

That covered ten minutes when few German fighters made contact and no one was hurt on either side. It sounds garbled and disjointed, telling none of the visual drama and conveying little of the profane urgency of the voices. Inside the blast walls of the Tangmere Ops. Room a loud-speaker purring with static clicked and spoke the metallic words of the pilots. Sitting at the radiophone, Woodhall had plenty to do, and so did the 'Beauty Chorus', the team of WAAFs pushing the pawns of the radar plots across the Ops table with long-handled paddles.

When the weather allowed, the pattern continued; there was less concentration by the Luftwaffe on shipping and ports while their bombers sought the destruction of airfields and industrial capacity by night raids on towns. 24th August saw the beginning of the third and most critical phase of the battle. Both Göring and Kesselring had overestimated the effect of the raids on airfields and believed their Intelligence reports that there were very few Spitfires left. The German fighter pilots, however, continued to run into Spitfires as well as Hurricanes in every quarter, and the vaunted Stukas were withdrawn as they were the most vulnerable aircraft when they strayed from fighter protection.

Again Manston was attacked, twice on the same day, its buildings destroyed, communications cut and the airfield pitted with bomb craters; it was evacuated and relegated to emergency use. Hornchurch and North Weald were bombed and 100 bombers and fighters attacked Southampton and Portsmouth. That night London was bombed, possibly due to a mistake in navigating for the Thames-side oil tanks. The following night a few British bombers got to Berlin to make a reciprocal gesture. The German raid on London was only a foretaste of what was to come in the Blitz, but even so, 1,000 civilians had been killed by the end of August.

12 Group squadrons were sometimes

Left: Last moment of a Junkers-88 caught by the gun camera of a Spitfire in the Battle of Britain

involved in the battle and the Group's tactics tended towards the bigger formations of two or more squadrons, to meet force with force. In 10 Group's area St Eval was attacked and a dummy airfield, equipped with a lighted flare path, was heavily bombed by the deluded Germans. The night raids over England were very harrowing for the population, but Blenheim and occasional Hurricane night fighters had little success against raiders. The airfields were continually attacked and Biggin Hill was almost put out of action after a succession of heavy raids. On 31st August the station was hit again and at Hornchurch three Spitfires were caught in a bomb-blast as they were taking off, but incredibly the pilots were only slightly injured. Two more Spitfires were destroyed at Hornchurch in a raid later that day, the day Fighter Command suffered its heaviest losses of thirty-nine fighters and fourteen pilots; the Germans lost forty-one aircraft and their crews.

Early in September the Luftwaffe began to seek the aircraft factories which they imagined were producing fighters so fast they were able to replace the enormous losses which the misled German Intelligence estimated the British had lost. The Wellington bomber factory was hit (Wellingtons had bombed Berlin) and Park ordered fighter cover for the Hurricane and Spitfire production centres. On 7th September, at Hitler's command, Göring ordered the beginning of the Blitz on London and during attacks which continued throughout the night 306 civilians were killed and 1,337 seriously injured Four nights later Buckingham Palace was damaged, and again on 13th September. On 7th September, Douglas Bader led two Hurricane squadrons and one Spitfire squadron to attack a large formation of Dorniers and Messerschmitts but only one Hurricane squadron intercepted, the other squadrons having failed to join up in time. From 11 Group, Spitfires intercepted some Me 109s at 25,000 feet while forty Dorniers below them at 20,000 feet were intercepted by two squadrons of Hurricanes, including the Polish No 303 Squadron led by Squadron Leader R G Kellett who attacked

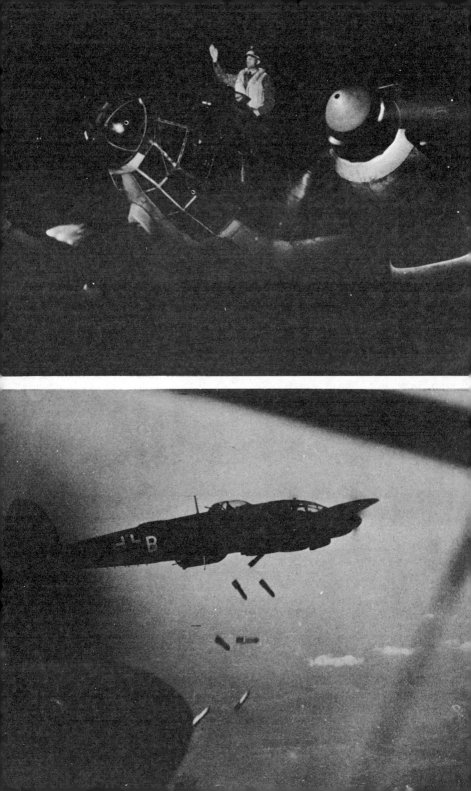

Left: A new phase of the Battle opens as a Heinkel III sets off for a night raid *Bottom left:* The day raids continue – a German bomber unloads a stick of bombs *Below:* The pilot boards his aircraft, whose engine has already been started by the ground crew *Bottom:* Spitfires on patrol

Left: Business as usual for bombed-out office workers in the middle of
the Blitz *Below:* Encouragement for rescue workers from the King, Queen
and Churchill *Bottom:* The ruins of St Mary-le-Bow in Cheapside

them, after diving from the sun at 400 mph, in line-abreast formation, firing until the range was almost point-blank. The RAF lost nineteen pilots and twenty-eight fighters, and the Germans lost forty-one bombers and fighters and their crews, including a Ju 88 shot down by an OTU instructor at Hawarden.

After the first night of the Blitz, Londoners expected the invasion to begin at any hour; the British GHQ Home Forces had issued the code word 'Cromwell', indicating that invasion was imminent and in southeast England the army prepared to 'fight on the beaches and fight in the fields'. On 3rd September, Hitler fixed the invasion date for 21st September, for by then he expected Göring's air forces to have completed their work. After the fighting on 15th September, however, this appeared to be impossible.

15th September was a hot sunny day, one of many in that 1940 summer, as the swarms of German fighters and bombers crossed the English coast and headed for London. At 11 Group's underground Operations Room, Winston Churchill had dropped in with his wife to make an informal visit to Keith Park. The Churchills were still there when the first reports came in of bombers and fighters approaching in large numbers from the south-east. (At North Weald station, General Strong and General Emmons of the USAAF and Admiral Gormley of the USN were making a visit to watch a fighter squadron station in action.) About fifty Heinkel bombers led larger formations of Dorniers; behind these were the faster Ju 88s and a few thousand feet above were the Messerschmitt fighters; altogether there were about 250 aircraft intent on burning out the heart of London.

Two squadrons of Spitfires made the first contact, over Kent, followed by another three squadrons, then by Hurricane squadrons south of London and then, in the first big-formation interception, by a five-squadron wing from 12 Group with Douglas Bader leading them. The first raid began at eleven am, a second developed soon after one pm, a third was made, ineffectually, on the Portland dockyards and the final raid was a swift attack by bomb-carrying Me 110s which just missed their objective, the Supermarine works at Woolston. The concerted attack on London was broken up and the bombs scattered over some dozen suburbs. One of the places damaged was the Queen's private apartments in Buckingham Palace. A Spitfire from No 609 Squadron shot the wing off a Dornier and the bullet-riddled wing fell outside a Pimlico public house, to the great joy of its patrons.

At the end of the day the claim was 185 German aircraft shot down but postwar figures are fifty-six actually brought down during daylight and four more that night. Many more dead and injured crew members were carried back in damaged bombers to France. Adolf Galland led his squadron of Me 109s over England that day and claimed shooting down four Hurricanes. The total losses to the RAF were twenty-six aircraft and thirteen pilots.

Leigh-Mallory and Bader, the 12 Group advocates of the idea of interception in Wing-strength (as opposed to the 11 Group idea of interception in Squadron-strength), were satisfied with the way that the five-squadron Wing they had put up had performed, although it had been the Spitfires that got among the bombers while the slower Hurricanes became entangled with the Me 109s. Bader was disappointed that they had not been ordered up earlier when they may have scored more than the Wing's claim of fifty-two destroyed and eight probables.

Once the enemy was sighted, Bader's fighters had split up and attacked, and once in the mêlée there had been, as always, no order, no direction and no pattern, for control was impossible in the whirling individual fights that developed. Some pilots had found themselves attacking one of the enemy alone, others escaping attacks by one or more of the enemy, and still others trying to avoid collisions and near-collisions. The whole fray had become a confusion of diving, turning, and climbing among friend and enemy until there was a chase and an escape, and then the sky could be empty of any other aircraft.

In a straight-out fight between a

number of Spitfires and an equal number of Me 109s, at the same height and with the sun neutral, either side could be the winner, depending on the determination, ability and experience of the pilots engaged. Such a fight would have been a rare occurrence throughout the war for one side or the other always had an advantage of height, surprise or numbers.

This day, 15th September, the day that saw the Germans severely beaten, is commemorated annually as Battle of Britain Day.

The daylight attacks eased up on the following two days but the night attacks on London continued. On 17th September Hitler postponed Operation 'Sea Lion'. Next day at nine am the radar screens shqwed a heavy build-up over Calais and on arrival over the south coast the enemy turned out to be mostly fighters, coming over south-east England at 20,000 feet. Seventeen RAF fighter squadrons attacked and drove them off. In the afternoon, about thirty Ju 88s ran into trouble when they were intercepted by Bader's wing from Duxford, or rather by the three Hurricane squadrons in the wing while the Spitfires stayed up high to ward off any supporting Me 110s. The Duxford Wing lost none and claimed thirty bombers shot down, six probables and two damaged; the postwar figures showed that only nineteen of the German force did not return from raiding that day. RAF pilots who fought in the battle believe now that the Germans must have 'rigged' their books for propaganda purposes. The British lost twelve fighters on this day and only three pilots killed.

19th September was the day that the concentrations of shipping for Operation 'Sea Lion' were dispersed as a result of increasing attacks by RAF bombers, and from this time onward the threat of invasion lessened. It was not until 12th October that Hitler decided to call off the whole thing until the spring of 1941 but by this date he had lost heart for the idea. The daylight raids became lighter as Hitler pinned his hopes on destroying Britain's capital and industrial centres on Merseyside and in the Midlands by continuous night bombing. On 26th September, Supermarine's

works at Woolston were hit by seventy tons of bombs and production was temporarily stopped. More than thirty people were killed and many more injured, three Spitfires on the line were destroyed, several others were damaged and Mitchell's partly-built bomber prototype (B12/36) was wrecked.

In two more major daylight raids the Luftwaffe again suffered severely. On 27th September, the first raid showed as blips on the radar screens at eight am as Me 110s carrying bombs and protected by Me 109s headed for London but were quickly intercepted and scattered. Two formations of bombers followed, but without fighter escort, and were cut up by 11 Group Hurricane and Spitfires. At eleven-thirty am two raids developed, one towards London, the other inland towards Bristol on the west coast. The German losses of fifty-five were almost double the twenty-eight aircraft lost by the RAF. On 30th September, the first raid was again soon after breakfast when one hundred fighters protected thirty bombers sweeping towards London; they were split up near Dungeness and did not reach London, nor did a following force of sixty aircraft. At eleven am there was a raid from the south-east by the two Messerschmitt types, although it did not get as far as the coast. At noon a raid was intercepted over Kent and this was a prelude to further minor raiding groups. Then came more than a hundred fighters and bombers, thirty of which reached London, and by four o'clock 180 were flying towards towns west of London. An aircraft factory at Yeovil was a target for another group of bombers and fighters, but the factory was missed. The official score for the day has been fixed at forty-seven German and twenty British aircraft shot down; twelve RAF pilots escaped unscathed.

The battle continued into October and more than ever the fighters were scrambled to climb to 20,000 to 30,000 feet to intercept fighters and fighter-bombers; the Me 109s as well as the Me 110s, were becoming bomb-carriers flying across from the Pas-de-Calais in less than thirty minutes from take-off, sometimes in large formations,

Above: Ground crew work on a Spitfire I of No 19 Squadron after the squadron's code letters on the fuselage have been changed to QV. Note the changed style of the roundel with a large matt yellow outer border to help recognition. *Below:* A German tries to keep his gun trained on a fast-moving Spitfire

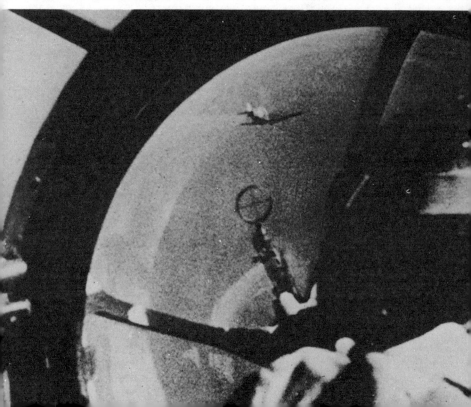

sometimes in pairs or singly, making interception very difficult. On 2nd October the Luftwaffe lost seventeen against a British loss of one; on the 4th October, it was twelve German for the loss of three British aircraft. The Me 109s performed better than Spitfires at heights over 20,000 feet, yet the German fighters were losing against British fighters which were coping with both bomber and fighter attacks. London continued to receive nightly attacks and not so large daylight raids by single fighter-bombers or small mixed groups. Of the airfields that were attacked throughout September and October, Biggin Hill received more attention than the others. A few of the enemy were intercepted over the sea but the rest crossed the coast and if they could not drop their bombs on a chosen target they dropped them anywhere – on suburbs, towns and villages, so that of the hundreds of German aircraft that flew over England every week, all caused some damage, however minor; the only result that Göring could hope to achieve was demoralisation of the population.

One of the worst raids on London was the night of 15th October, a raid which began as the full moon rose in the evening. There had been four minor raids during the day and Waterloo Station had been hit and almost completely closed down. That night there were over 900 fires in London; over 400 civilian dead and 800 severely injured were counted the next morning. The Italians asked the Germans to allow them to join in on the comparatively safe night bombing operations and their first raid was made, by fifteen Fiat bombers, over Harwich. But, after all these attacks, the civilians of London, of Merseyside, of the dockyard areas and of the numerous towns and villages that suffered the ruthless, indiscriminate raids were not demoralised; Britain's supplies were interrupted but she was not cut off as completely as Göring had hoped, and Fighter Command was just as strong at the end of October as when the battle began in July.

As winter set in, the Luftwaffe continued its night bombing. Civilian casualties for October, November and December were 14,715 killed and 20,141 seriously injured. The daylight raids were light and infrequent, enabling Fighter Command to rest its pilots and re-equip squadrons. Spitfire IIs were beginning to replace Mk Is which were going to OTUs where trainee fighter pilots could benefit from the lessons learnt in the recent combats.

The RAF victory was dry cut and positive. Hermann Göring's Luftwaffe had not only been prevented from destroying Dowding's Fighter Command, they had lost the greater number of aircraft and a larger proportion of air crews. The Germans lost over 1,700 aircraft to the RAF's 900, including those destroyed on the ground. More than 500 RAF pilots were killed with many more injured. Of those killed, over 400 were Britons; the others were Canadians, Australians, New Zealanders, South Africans, Poles, Czechs, Free French, Belgians and 'neutral' Americans.

Of the 'Few', fewer still were good shots. Five of the top scorers shot down over a hundred enemy aircraft between them, while at the other end of the scale some did not score one hit in the same period. Justly, they too gave valuable service, as Number Twos, who could quarter the skies and give warnings. The more pilots fought, the more experience they gained in shooting and flying, the more likely they would be to inflict some damage and to live through future battles.

Spitfires influenced the course of the Battle of Britain by providing an extra strength which the Germans soon noted. If there had only been the formidable but limited Hurricanes opposing them, the Germans might have persisted in their attacks against the airfields, radar stations and aircraft factories. The beneficial effect of the Spitfire might be compared with Rommel's successes won in the desert with the help of his superior 88 mm anti-aircraft gun turned tank-buster.

The quality of the Spitfire raised urgent demands from the Luftwaffe for improved fighters and the race to provide better machines continued until the end of the war.

Marks II-V

It is surprising that the RAF had not made attacks on the German airfields near the French coast with fighters during the Battle of Britain. It was necessary to conserve Spitfires and Hurricanes for defence, but two other fighter types, which were no match in a dogfight for Me 109s, could have been effective in low-level sweeps: the Boulton-Paul Defiant, armed with its four Browning 0.303 inch machine gun turret, and the slower twin-engined Bristol Blenheim armed with four Brownings in a ventral pack, another Browning in the port wing and a Vickers K gun in a dorsal turret. Low level attacks across the Channel, or by using cloud cover for surprise attacks, could have resulted in the destruction or damage of numerous German bombers and fighters, thereby easing the task of the Spitfires and Hurricanes.

During the early winter of 1940, offensives were planned, to utilise the more agile fighters in sweeps against the Luftwaffe in Occupied France, against aircraft in the air and on the ground, against airfields, ports, shipping and transport. These were ambitious but logical and practical plans for the further utilisation of a force which had just finished fighting for its existence but needed only rest before its full strength was restored. The tactics of hunters alter drastically when they become the hunted, and the change in the fortunes of the aerial battles which began in 1941 improved the morale of the British, civilians and forces alike; on the German side the civilian population was misinformed but the occupied countries were stimulated to resist when they could see for themselves that Britain was fighting back. The German aircraft industry was also galvanised into the rapid development of fighters superior to the Spitfire, development which the expected early end of the war had reduced to a low priority.

Whereas Messerschmitts suffered lack of range in flights over England, the Germans now had less miles to fly to engage the British, whose aircraft were restricted in use of full throttle and whose pilots would be captured if forced to bale out over France or the French side of the Channel – exactly the opposite of the situation during the Battle of Britain. Fighter Command's primary weapon in this phase was the Spitfire II. There was very little difference between the two marks: the Mk II had a Merlin XII of 1,150 hp, related to the Merlin III but with a Coffman starter; it was slower in maximum and cruising speeds yet could climb faster to 20,000 feet (in seven minutes) and reach 32,800 feet because of the efficiency of its Rotol three-blade Jablo constant-speed airscrew. In this mark, more 'B' wings with four machine guns and two cannon were fitted. The cannon were drum-fed and to fit the guns into the slender wing a small blister was raised on top of the wing to provide the necessary extra space.

Of the 920 Mk IIs built, 170 were completed as IIBs which were not very popular at first because of the poor results obtained by No 19 Squadron testing the cannon in combat: that stoppages were frequent is shown by the fact that on one occasion six out of seven Mk IIBs suffered cannon stoppages. The Air Ministry had decided to manufacture Hispano 20mm cannon in 1939 and a factory for the purpose was built at Newcastle-under-Lyme with early production planned for 750 per month.

The armour of the Mk II gave pilot protection from seat to head, and protected the glycol header tank and the top fuel tank, which could not be made self-sealing without spoiling the aircraft's streamlining. Weight of the armour was seventy-three pounds.

In December 1940, with the beginning of the new offensive operations, extra range was sought for the fighters. A Spitfire's potential in damaging enemy aircraft – and that was the main purpose of the new year sweeps – lay in the time spent over France, but the eighty-five gallons carried internally allowed for less than two hours' fast cruising and a few minutes of combat. At first, range was improved by installing a forty gallon tank in the port wing, but then jettisonable thirty, forty-five or ninety gallon tanks were made in a 'slipper' form to

Left: New armament for the Spitfire – a Mk IIB with two 20mm Hispano cannon and four machine guns

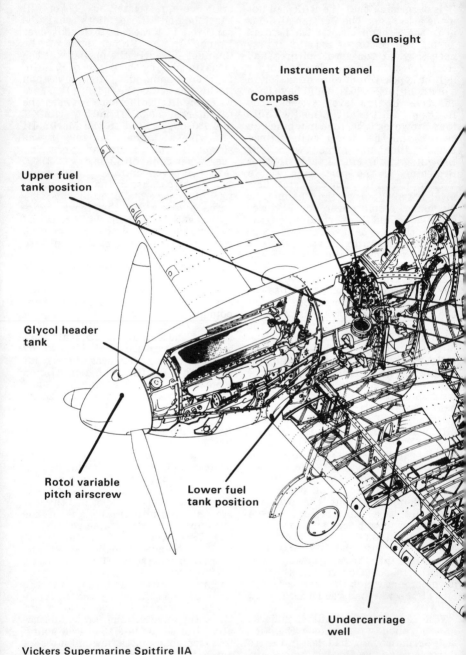

Gunsight

Instrument panel

Compass

Upper fuel
tank position

Glycol header
tank

Rotol variable
pitch airscrew

Lower fuel
tank position

Undercarriage
well

Vickers Supermarine Spitfire IIA
Engine: Rolls-Royce Merlin XII, 1,150 hp *Armament:* Eight .303-inch Browning
machine guns with 350 rounds per gun *Maximum speed:* 357 mph at 17,000 feet
Initial climb rate: 2,600 feet per minute *Ceiling:* 32,800 feet *Range:* 395 miles
Weight empty: 4,885 lbs *Weight loaded:* 6,275 lbs *Span:* 36 feet 10 inches
Length: 29 feet 11 inches

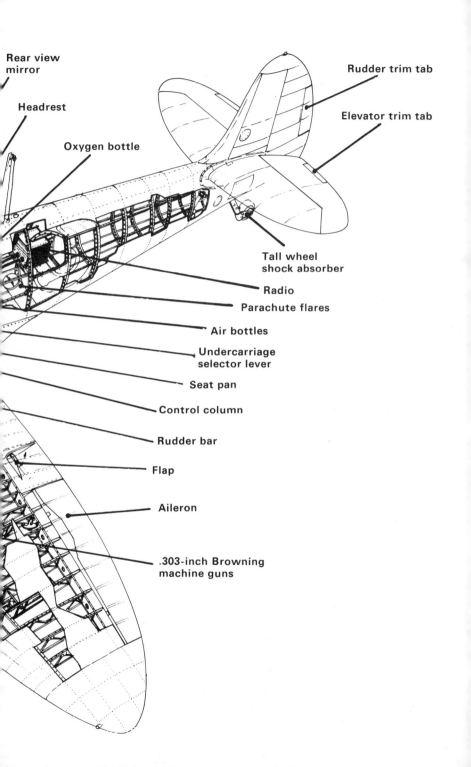

Rear view mirror

Headrest

Oxygen bottle

Rudder trim tab

Elevator trim tab

Tail wheel shock absorber

Radio

Parachute flares

Air bottles

Undercarriage selector lever

Seat pan

Control column

Rudder bar

Flap

Aileron

.303-inch Browning machine guns

fit flush under the fuselage section.

The practice was to take off on the main tanks, change over to the drop-tank (once there was sufficient height to bale out, glide down or turn over to the main tanks if a fuel stoppage occurred) and drop the tanks once the enemy was sighted or the auxiliary fuel contained in them was used. Mark IIs, all 920 of which were made at the Castle Bromwich factory, were also among the first Air-Sea-Rescue Spitfires to go into service, as Spitfire IICs. (This is the only example of a suffix to a mark number not referring to the armament of the Spitfire. In this case, the Spitfire IIA and B had appeared, and when this new model appeared, logic dictated that it be called the IIC. 'C' wings were in service by this time, but this was ignored. When role prefixes came into use, the IIC became the ASR II, the initials standing for Air-Sea-Rescue.) They were fitted with two smoke bombs and two chutes in the rear fuselage for a small dinghy and a food container, to be dropped by parachute to airmen in the sea. With many bombers, fighter-bombers and fighters using the cross-Channel routes it was imperative for Fighter Command to improve the sea rescue facilities and eventually six ASR squadrons were in service.

New terms had come into the RAF language with the new ideas for offence. Bader's big wing formation was called a 'Balbo' – after the prewar Italian Air-Marshal Italo Balbo who led large formations on long flights – and there were 'Beehives' of fighters swarmed protectively around bombers, 'Rhubarbs' of one or more fighters making fast offensive sweeps into enemy territory, and 'Circuses' (sweeps) of multi-role fighters. The most exciting trip was a 'Rhubarb', trouble-seeking, often at low level where the scenery rushed past and the true speed of a fighter was sensed, and without the inhibiting unwieldiness of a large formation. To the keen and aggressive pilots, the chance to go out chasing 'Huns' was heaven-sent. The number of fighter squadrons on operations (some were resting or working up) was increasing but there was plenty of action for all as the offensives and German low-level in-

truders increased in number with the approach of summer.

One British advantage was still the superiority of their radar which guided them and scanned the skies for the enemy. The following extract from *Reach for the Sky* is of an R/T conversation with the controller, Wing-Commander Woodhall, when Bader was leader of the Tangmere Wing of Spitfires in 1941:

"On the way across no one broke radio silence till they were nearly over the French coast where the Germans could see them. Then it was usually Bader:

'O.K., Green Line Bus (the wing). Pull your corks out. You O.K., Ken?'

'O.K., D. B. In position. (Holden, leader of 610 Squadron.)

'You O.K. Stan? Where the hell are you? I can't see you.'

'O.K., D. B. Keep your cork in. I'm here.' (From Stan Turner leading 145 Squadron, up sun.)

'Hallo, Woodie, any trade in sight?'

'Hallo, Dogsbody. Beetle (Woodhall) answering. Seems to be a strong reaction building up over the Big Wood (St Omer). About thirty or forty plus gaining altitude to the east of the objective. I am watching them. That's all for now.'

'Soon Woodhall again: "Hallo, Dogsbody. The 109s over the Big Wood are climbing south. Looks as though they might be trying to come in down-sun on your right flank.'

'O.K., Woody.'

'A few minutes silence and then:

'Hallo, Dogsbody. If you look about three o'clock above I think you'll see what you're looking for.'

It was uncanny how accurate he was. Usually in a few moments someone saw them sliding into sun-ambush, looking against the sky like a stream of silver fish darting in a ragged straggle through a pool. They broke into small packs to come in from many angles, and Bader had his eyes everywhere, assessing, manoeuvring the wing, warning, detaching sections, reorganising, picking the moment to lunge and start the roaring, whirling frenzy."

Clashes rarely lasted more than a few minutes, with the Me 109s flying off as if they were at a disadvantage either by inferior height or turning

Top: **One of the two Mk IIIs in use as an engine test-bed**
Above: **The Me-109, still the Spitfire's great enemy**

abilities and with the Spitfires not staying long as their combat endurance at this range was very limited. If they could not or would not join up, stragglers were easy meat and even 'tail-end Charlies' were frequently shot down unless they were superbly alert – and too many were not.

Mark Is remained in service after the IIs were introduced, the latter going to the more active stations where squadrons converted from the old to the new as they moved from rest stations to operations. As operational training expanded, Mk Is were flown to OTUs and for a few months the Mk IIs held the fort and intruded against the enemy. The higher ceiling and better rate of climb, and the fact that they were all newer, made the Mk II a better fighting aircraft, but they were not good enough to take on superior numbers of the new Me 109F (Bf 109F-1), the first of which to

be shot down over Britain fell on 11th May 1941, or another new fighter, the Focke-Wulf Fw 190A-2, which went into service with Adolf Galland's *Jagdgeschwader* (JG) 26 on airfields near the French coast.

The German production of two superior fighters could have been more serious had not Mitchell's basic design been adaptable for further modifications to the airframe to accommodate more powerful engines. The next Spitfire to be produced in large quantity was the Mk V which also found the developing Me 109 and Fw 190 types too fast. Next in the development of the Spitfire came the Mks III and IV, which were both attempts to utilise more powerful engines in the standard Spitfire airframe. Two Mark IIIs were built in 1940, equipped with Merlin XXs of 1,390 hp, retractable tailwheels and clipped wings. (They were the first Spitfires to have a clipped wing.) Only two were built. The Spitfire IV was a new departure in the development of the Spitfire, as it was fitted with a larger Rolls-Royce 1,735 hp engine, the Griffon. It became a test machine for later marks. The PR IV was similar to the Mk V and is described in the section on Photographic Reconaissance Spitfires.

Fighter-versus-fighter combat rarely continued until one side had been annihilated and usually lasted only a few minutes – i.e. until the losers broke away; the accumulated losses of either side were the determining factors and in the long run it was the fastest and the highest that would come out on top. When the Luftwaffe fighter squadrons received the new Me 109Fs in the spring of 1941, they possessed an aircraft markedly superior, except in turning, to the Spitfire II. Thus in the battles of attrition the Me 109F had the advantage to climb, attack and then dive safely away. The Spitfire only succeeded against this form of attack by facing the enemy and being able to out-turn him in a dogfight; when the Spitfire had the advantage of height the Messerschmitt was at a disadvantage all round in the early stages of the combat for it could not escape quickly enough in a dive initially and the Spitfire could easily follow it in a turn. This is a simplification of what happened but it was usually the first passes which caused the damage, when pilots had a clear idea of what was happening; soon afterwards even the most experienced found themselves in a confusion of milling aeroplanes and weaving, waggling wings, having to look below, left, right, above, into the mirror, look around, waggle, peer, check position and instruments and look into the sun. The one that got you was the one you did not see – and he was usually above and behind or below and behind, or hidden by the brilliance of the sun.

Meanwhile, the war was taking on another look, as the German forces turned on the Russian giant. Hitler's Operation 'Barbarossa' (the invasion of Russia), delayed by the German invasion of Yugoslavia and the necessity of giving support to the beaten Italian army in Greece, began on 22nd June 1941, the mighty German armies and air forces crossing the Russian frontier to begin what was at first a rapid, devastating advance. The change in the war brought relief to London, Merseyside, Plymouth, Devonport and other areas which had suffered from heavy night bombing through the winter and into the 1941 summer. It was not until May/June that RAF radar-equipped nightfighters began to take a heavier toll of the raiders. For the rest of the year the Luftwaffe was occupied on the Russian front and British cities and industry enjoyed a reprieve.

The Spitfire V came into service in this period. It was a compromise aircraft like the Mk II, but became the most numerous of all Spitfire types: ninety-four Mk VAs armed with eight machine guns, 3,923 Mk VBs with two cannon and four machine guns, and 2,447 Mk VCs fitted with the new Universal 'C' wing which provided for 'A' or 'B' wing armament and, instead of the sixty-round drum which previously fed the cannon, 120-round belts were fitted in bins. Of the 6,479 built at the Supermarine, Castle Bromwich and Westland works, about half were delivered in 1941. The only distinguishing exterior feature for fleeting identification was the much bigger undernose with its carburettor intake just behind the propeller on the tropical type.

Rolls-Royce had stepped up the power of the Merlin to 1,415 hp at 19,000 feet and 1,470 hp at 16,000 feet in the Merlin 45s and 46s powering most Mark Vs.

Another version of the 45 engine was the 45M, which had the impeller blades of the supercharger 'cropped' to give an extra 15 hp at low altitudes, and this gave the Spitfire LF (Low-altitude Fighter) V a top speed of 357 mph at 6,000 feet. Merlins 50 and 50A, versions of the 45, and the 50M cropped version of the 50 were also fitted to Mk Vs. Spitfire variations were now becoming complicated; there were three types of wings and engines with three different altitude ratings the result being that the various types were given prefixes 'LF' for low altitude, 'F' for medium altitude and 'HF' for high altitude. The majority of, but not all, LF models had two feet and four inches clipped from each wing tip for faster aileron reaction at lower levels. Actually, the only high-altitude Mk Vs were three unofficially modified in service by No 103 Mainten-

Vickers Supermarine Spitfire VB (71 Eagle Squadron, May 1942)
Engine: Rolls-Royce Merlin 45, 45M, 46, 50, 50A, 50M or 56, 1,470 hp – 1,585 hp
Armament: Two 20mm Hispano cannon with 120 rounds per gun and
four .303-inch Browning machine guns with 350 rounds per gun, plus one
500 lbs or two 250 lbs bombs *Maximum speed:* 369 mph at 19,500 feet
Initial climb rate: 4,750 feet per minute *Ceiling:* 35,500 feet
Range: 470 miles normal, c. 1,000 miles max *Weight empty:* 5,065 lbs
Weight loaded: 6,785 lbs *Span:* 36 feet 10 inches *Length:* 29 feet 11 inches

ance Unit at Aboukir in Egypt where many practical aircraft modifications were carried out to suit desert conditions. The three Mk VC specials were given elongated wings, two 0.5 inch guns instead of the usual four guns and two cannon, four-blade airscrews and modified carburettors. The purpose of all this work was to get the Spitfires up over 40,000 feet to deal with Ju 86P reconnaissance aircraft previously immune from interception. When a Merlin 61 engine of 1,565 hp became available, one of the VCs was fitted with the more powerful engine and two cannon to go Junkers-hunting in the rarefied heights above Egypt.

The few Mk VAs built had a maximum speed of 376 mph at 19,500 feet, while the Mk VBs reached 369 mph at that height and the Mk VC 374 mph at 13,000 feet. The VB and VC could carry two 250-pound or one 500-pound bombs. Service ceiling varied from 35,500 feet for the LF VB to 37,000 feet for the F VC. Pilots referred to the hotted-up clipped-wing version as 'clipped, cropped and clapped' because of the clipping of the wings, the cropping of the supercharger impeller blades, and its sluggishness at 10,000 feet (the height they often escorted bombers on raids across the Channel); 'clapped' usually described the state of the boosted engines after a very limited life.

Windscreen de-icing, improved hood-jettisoning mechanism, armour weight increased to 152 pounds, reinforced longerons, extended horn balances on the elevators and metal-covered ailerons with sharp trailing edges were the main modifications introduced during the long-term production of Mk Vs. The ailerons were effective in improving the rolling rate by overcoming the tendency to aileron-stick at high speeds. The Mk VC had its wheels set two inches further forward to reduce a tendency to nose-over when taxiing in mud or over rocky fields, and the undercarriage was strengthened. Short fairing stubs in the 'C' wings covered the spare cannon ports.

For service in desert and tropical regions a special carburettor air filter was fitted, its intake moved further forward in a large housing under the engine cowling. Most Mk Vs were 'tropicalised' with the Vokes Multi-Vee filter to prevent the entry of sand from the desert, dust from dry or earthen airfields and powdered coral from island strips (matter which could reduce the life of a less efficiently filtered engine, by wearing out bearings and cylinder walls, to about thirty hours) entering the engine. Engine performance varied because of differences in carburettor systems, supercharger gear ratios, airscrew reduction and gearbox drives. By June, 1941, a thousand Mk Vs had been built and for the next year, whether 'sweeping' over France or defending at home, they were too hard-pressed to maintain RAF fighter superiority over the improving Messerschmitts and Focke-Wulfs.

Spitfire II of No 611 Squadron

Spitfire V's in vic formation

Fighters were ideal for strafing, their speed bringing them to their targets before the AA-gunners had realised it, then away from the vicious 'flak', which pilots began to fear more than enemy fighters. In the pre-rocket days, twin or quadruple cannon fire was the most effective weapon against locomotives, aircraft on the ground, motor vehicles, tanks, small ships and factories. When Fighter Command ordered the intruder operations, cannon-firing Spitfires caused widespread havoc among these objectives. Control staff heard the new slant of leaders' instructions in the air – instead of the familiar 'Bandits ten o'clock above' it could be 'Train ten o'clock below' as a 'Rhubarb' flight swooped down to strafe an enemy locomotive. Flak was the main danger but there were also hazardous objects like power cables to watch out for, while it was still necessary to keep an alert eye on the skies above. For these attacks, armourers filled the belts with a combination of tracer, explosive and armour-piercing shells and bullets, and every second cannon shell was an incendiary.

Two famous wing-leaders, Bader and Tuck, flew their last sorties in Mk Vs. On a cloudy day in January 1941, Bob Stanford Tuck led his No Two, a Canadian named Harley, on a 'Rhubarb' shoot-up of an alcohol distillery in the Le Touquet district in northern France – flying low across the Channel and across the French fields, below the German radar and passing AA batteries too fast for the surprised gunners to lay their weapons on the fighters. Near the target they pulled up into cloud and when they were nearing shooting distance they dived down to set the earth aflame with exploding, burning liquid as the cannon shells hit. After this they meandered along until they spotted a locomotive, blew it up, but then found themselves in a valley thick with cross-firing AA guns. Tuck's Spitfire was hit:

'Several shots smacked into the belly. One shell came right up through the sump, through the cooling system, and everything stopped dead. She started to belch black smoke, glycol and all sorts of filth. The windscreen was covered in oil, so I had to slam

back the canopy and stick my head outside.'

'When they kept pouring shells at me, I had a terrific urge to climb her before the speed fell too low, but I knew the moment I got on to the skyline they'd have me like a box of birds.'

With his motor dead he dived and glided towards a long field for a fast belly landing – into the fire from an AA battery.

'He shoved the stick forward, lined up his sight – and by sheer force of habit checked the turn-and-bank indicator. Then he fired his last, short burst . . . He was still doing 120 but he was running out of field, so immediately he took a deep breath, put the stick forward and set her down . . . struggled out of his harness and clambered on to the wing. A few yards away the gun lorry lay shattered and smoking, the mangled bodies of its crew strewn around it . . . From both sides of the field, grey figures were running towards him. There was no hope of avoiding them. "The bastards will lynch me now," he thought bitterly.'

But no; the Germans' anger, their insults and kicking ceased and then changed to laughter as they pointed out to him the barrel of one of the multiple 20mm flak cannon split by a shot down the barrel by one of Tuck's shells. And they congratulated him on his good shooting! After making many attempts, Tuck eventually escaped from a POW camp in Poland to further strange experiences with Russian forces. His story, from which the above extracts have been taken, was written by Larry Forrester and entitled *Fly For Your Life*.

Douglas Bader had the qualities of one of the many types of fighter pilots – the athlete type; alert, quick reflexes, an excellent sense of teamwork and positive leadership. A regular officer, he was a member of the élite aerobatic team which flew Gloster Gamecocks at the 1931 Hendon Air Display and that year he was also chosen to play rugby for England. However, before he could win his England cap, he crashed while demon-

Wing-Commander Robert Stanford-Tuck, one of the highest scoring pilots of the early war years

Sub-Lieutenant Colin Hodgkinson,

strating a slow roll low across the Woodley Aerodrome near Reading. He was taken from his wrecked Bristol Bulldog with his legs so badly injured that they had to be amputated. He only just survived the operations and when he recovered he chose to be invalided out of the RAF rather than accept a ground job. When war broke out, he pestered the Air Ministry until they agreed to take him back on flying duties, depending on a medical check-up and a test of his ability to fly with two artificial legs – which he had mastered so amazingly well that he could not only walk and dance but also play an eighteen-hole round of golf.

It was August, a year after the Battle of Britain. Leigh-Mallory had taken over 11 Group from Park, Sholto Douglas had taken over Fighter Command from Dowding – the first man ever to win a major air battle – and Bader was commanding the Tangmere Spitfire wing. The squadrons had been re-equipped with Mk VBs and since Bader had an aversion to the cannon armament he was given a Mk VA. In his last action, the wing was to join up with a 'Beehive' over Lille and knock down anything that came their way. The wing ran into German fighters as it crossed the French coast, Bader misjudged his first attack then got two Me 109s in a lone attack against six of them. The end came soon afterwards – a colliding Me 109 chopped off his fuselage from tail to radio mast and Bader, with great difficulty, eased himself out of the spiralling remains which were falling at over 400 mph; he got one leg out but the other was caught up in the cockpit until the strap broke and he parted from the metal leg. He pulled the ripcord and floated down to land painfully on the stump of one leg and his remaining artificial leg. Bader escaped once and was caught, made many more attempts to get away and was such an unruly POW that his captors finally sent him to the notorious 'escape proof' Colditz Castle in the centre of Germany. In his short fighting war he had shot down thirty enemy aircraft, twenty-two-and-a-half of which were officially confirmed.

In 1942 another legless RAF pilot got

The RAF's first big test after the Battle of Britain – the escape from Brest of *Scharnhorst* and *Gneisenau*

back into flying and he too flew Spitfires. This 'tin legs' pilot was Colin Hodgkinson, who feared that if he were shot down and forced to bail out into the sea his artificial legs would fill with water and pull him under before he could inflate his dinghy, so he filled his legs with ping-pong balls, and thought he was being attacked when he heard explosions at high altitude – in fact the ping-pong balls were bursting as a result of the reduced atmospheric pressure.

In a big clash with Luftwaffe fighters above the escaping *Scharnhorst*, *Gneisenau* and *Prinz Eugen*, Fw 190s proved superior to the Mk Vs except in turning and even that margin was small. No 452 Squadron, RAAF, was one of the squadrons involved and instead of finding German aircraft, their leader, the intrepid 'Bluey' Truscott, spotted what he thought at first to be a transport sailing through the haze – it was not until the squadron began their attack that he realised that it was a flak-filled destroyer. However, the twelve Spitfires were committed and Truscott led them at high speed into the concentrated fire from the ship's guns. The surprise of the attack, and luck, got the aircraft through and they raked the destroyer from stem to stern, attacked again and the enemy guns were silenced before the squadron flew away intact. It was the first successful fighter attack against an enemy destroyer. A couple of years later, Truscott was to lead his fighter squadron, No 76,

American pilots scramble to their Mk VBs supplied under reverse Lend-Lease to the USAAF

RAAF, to attack a Japanese destroyer during the epic Kittyhawk defence of Milne Bay in New Guinea.

By the middle of 1942 there were fifty-nine squadrons in Britain equipped with Mk Vs, and forty-two of them were involved in the mass fighter cover cover for the Dieppe raid during which the first USAAF squadron equipped with Spitfires – the 307th of the 31st Fighter Group – flew into action.

The first American pilots to fly Spitfires were, of course, the several who flew in the Battle of Britain as volunteers: A G Donahue, W M L Fiske, P H Leckrone, V C Keough, A B Mamedoff and E G Tobin, the last three leaving No 609 Squadron in October 1940 to become the first pilots of the newly formed Eagle Squadron (No 71) at Church Fenton in Yorkshire. It was not until September the following year that the squadron went into action, flying Mk Vs from Martlesham Heath and North Weald on sweeps across France. A second Eagle Squadron (No 121) was formed in May and their first operation was a 'Rhubarb' in Mk Vs in November. No 133 was the third American squadron formed in the RAF, also flying Mk Vs, and they repeated No 121's record by getting an Fw 190 as their first kill.

The other two squadrons of the USAAF 31st Fighter Group were also equipped with Mk Vs and when the 52nd Fighter Group arrived in England they were re-equipped with Mk Vs after losing six out of twelve P-39 Airacobras in a sweep in July 1942. In September, the three Eagle Squadrons changed uniforms and flags but not their Spitfires and became the 334th, 335th and 336th Squadrons of the US Eighth Air Force's 4th Fighter Group. Four other American squadrons, members of the 67th Observation Group, flew Mk VBs, a few of which were used for training by the 13th Reconnaissance Squadron.

OTU trainees flew dual with instructors who had been in action, and lectures were given on fighting tactics. Experiences of fighting tactics were examined while the 'hangar doors' were ever open in the squadron messes and keen leaders like Johnson, Bader, Deere, Tuck, Caldwell, Finucane and the many others encouraged their pilots to discuss the problems and make suggestions. During the battle the strategic moves were left to Air-Chief-Marshal Sir Hugh Dowding and his staff at Fighter Command HQ while tactical control was in the hands of officers commanding Groups, and these officers worked them out with their wing and squadron leaders.

The main problem in that period was the tightness of the formations, the peacetime standards and practice of fighter-training restricting the ability to attack and defend. The discussions of service pilots engendered a different system of looser formations: instead of flying in vics of three, sections flew in fours, roughly line-abreast – 'fingers four' as they were called, the fingertips of a hand illustrating the relative position of the flight leader, with his Number Two on one side and on the other the leader of the other pair in the 'four', whose Number Two formated on the further side of him. Thus the four could break up into two pairs with two leaders covered by their Number Twos. Spaced up to fifty yards apart, the four pilots were free to manoeuvre, but could quickly form into line-astern, needed to devote less attention to keeping formation and were better able to keep a constant lookout. These were the tactical formations learned and practised in the First World War, neglected until necessity and observation of German tactics broke the ties with peacetime operational training.

In pair formations, leaders were in a much better position to make more kills than their 'wing men' – as Ameri-cans dubbed their Number Twos – but teamwork was an essential part of aerial combat and at times there were plenty of black crosses around for everyone to shoot at.

A watch on the sky was maintained by scanning from one side to the other, above and below, with regular 'clearing' of wings, tail and nose by skidding with rudder to expose those parts hidden by them. In squadron formations one or two 'tail-end Charlies' were stationed at the rear to cross back and forth to watch for bandits astern. The sun was a dangerous blind spot from where the enemy came at every opportunity; eventually, on the control room tables, the sun was plotted and whenever possible the squadrons were directed on interceptions to a position between sun and enemy.

The experiences of the aces would be passed on to trainees, who could not really exhibit during training the instinct and common sense they would have to possess and use in combat. Learning how to stay alive was as important as learning how to shoot down the opposition, and probably the most important manoeuvre was avoiding the fire of an enemy attacking from behind. Clive Caldwell was for a time Chief Flying Instructor

Group-Captain A G 'Sailor'
Malan, third on the list of RAF aces
with 35 victories

of an OTU and his experience was a unique record against German, Italian, Vichy French and Japanese fighters. He brought down at least forty aircraft, although his official score is less, at twenty-eight-and-a-half. His advice for getting away from an enemy fighter – any enemy fighter – in that deadly rear position was to break violently, shoving 'everything into one corner' even though it hurt.

Breaking in this way, kicking on the rudder pedal as far as it would go, at the same time pushing the stick to the same side and forward, both actions simultaneously and quickly, hastened by a healthy sense of panic, threw the Spitfire's nose and wing down into a spiral, the pilot being flung to one side and tight up into his straps with the blood rushing to his head so that he was blinded in a 'red-out' of negative 'G' – the opposite of 'black-out', when the blood rushes toward the feet. This action left the enemy's bullets in space and was impossible for him to follow closely – he would follow but there was no necessity for him to hurt himself and his manoeuvres would be slower. If the Spitfire continued on its spiral dive it would again be a sitting target, particularly with a partly-dazed pilot at the controls, and the enemy needed only to make a normal dive to line up his sights for another shot. The next move, after a slow count of three, was to bring the controls back to centre and pull hard on the stick, clearing the red from the eyes but going into a blackout as the steep pull-out produced a positive 'G'. Continuing to climb with the impetus of a dive to increase its speed, and the pilot's vision returning to normal, the Spitfire could arrive in a position higher than that of the enemy.

Another famous leader, Adolf 'Sailor' Malan, a South African who joined the RAF before the war, had these ten rules printed for distribution when he was Commander of No 61 OTU in 1942:

'1. Wait until you see the whites of his eyes. Fire short bursts of 1 or 2 seconds and only when your sights are definitely "ON".

2. Whilst shooting think of nothing else; brace the whole of your body; have both hands on the stick; concentrate on your ring sight.

3. Always keep a sharp lookout. "Keep your fingers out!"

4. Height gives *You* the initiative.

5. Always turn and face the attack.

6. Make your decisions promptly. It is better to act quickly even though your tactics are not the best.

7. Never fly straight and level for more than thirty seconds in the combat area.

8. When diving to attack always leave a proportion of your formation above to act as top guard.

9. *Initiative, aggression, air discipline*, and TEAM WORK are the words that MEAN something in Air Fighting.

10. Go in quickly – Punch hard – Get out!'

Baling out of a Spitfire was not too difficult. In emergencies, with flames or smoke in the cockpit or with controls shot away or with chunks of aeroplane missing, pilots have got out in all kinds of position. Simply going over the side might mean crashing into the elevators or fin but it was the instinctive way – pushing back the hood, releasing safety harness and oxygen tube, pulling out the radio plug, jumping and counting to ten (if there was enough height) before pulling the ripcord. The safest way was to trim the elevator tab fully forward, roll the Spitfire over on to its back, let the stick go and jump while the aircraft bunted (began an outside or inverted loop), giving an extra push to the pilot's jump.

Occasionally there was not enough height to bale out and pilots were forced to belly-land or ditch in the sea. The Spitfire went into water as happily as a seal and gave the pilot perhaps two or three seconds to get out. Some of those who survived a ditching got out so deep that the colour of the water was changing from green to black, or from the sea bottom as did one pilot in Darwin Harbour. Baling out was imperative if a Spitfire became unflyable over water and the pilot wished to live to join the exclusive Goldfish Club and wear its little gold emblem. Another club, the Caterpillar, was for pilots returned from being shot down over enemy territory.

Spitfires abroad

When Rommel's Afrika Korps came to the aid of the defeated Italian armies in North Africa and German Panzers pushed the British and Commonwealth forces back through Libya and threatened Egypt, and Greece and Crete had been occupied, the little island of Malta was the most important strategic point in the Mediterranean between Gibraltar and Alexandria. Mussolini's bombers and fighters first raided Malta on 11th June 1940, the day after Italy declared war on Britain, and continued to mount increasing raids against Valetta's harbour, shipping and airfields in an effort to neutralise the island so that it could be invaded. At first, the island's only fighter defence was a flight of four Sea Gladiator biplanes borrowed by the RAF from the Navy. Dogfights against the Fiat CR 42 biplanes looked like re-enactments of actions from the Great War as they flew their tight circles, loops and Immelman turns, machine guns chattering at heights low enough for watchers on the ground to observe. Some Italian pilots actually believed that perfectly executed aerobatics would enable them to out-fly and so out-fight the Gladiator pilots; Italians were knocked down, and no doubt surprised, in the middle of perfect slow rolls while their antagonists simply flew straight and level behind and fired. Three of the Gladiators survived for a time against overwhelming odds. They were called 'Faith', 'Hope' and 'Charity' by the Maltese and were kept flying by using bits and pieces from the fourth, which had crashed. There was only one left, a many times repaired and patched Gladiator, when several Hurricanes were brought over from Egypt.

Early in 1942 it seemed that Malta was doomed unless the defences were reinforced with modern fighters, and if Malta were to fall the whole Allied campaign in North Africa would be in jeopardy. Fighters were in short supply in the desert war where Me 109s outclassed the Hurricanes and Curtiss Kittyhawks; the Middle East Air Force urgently asked for Spitfires

Left: **Spitfire VC (tropicalised) on Malta. The large filter under the nose keeps out the fine dust**

for both Malta (which was vitally necessary as a bomber base for attacks against Axis shipping and airfields and for future operations against Sicily and Italy) and for the Western Desert where Rommel had attacked in strength in January. The first half of 1942 was the worst part of the war for the Allies, with the Japanese going on from success to success at Rangoon and Bataan, Australia threatened, the Germans pushing the Russians off the Kerch Peninsula and old towns in England suffering under the Luftwaffe's 'Baedeker' raids.

The only way to ship supplies and Spitfires to Malta was either by the long, hazardous route round the Cape or by the short, even more hazardous, route through the Straits of Gibraltar which were under constant surveillance by Axis agents in Algeciras in Spain, risking bombs, shells and torpedoes from Axis aircraft, submarines and warships. Thousands of tons of shipping loaded with valuable cargoes for North Africa and Malta had been sent to the bottom of the Mediterranean and the safest way to get the fighters out was by aircraft carrier. Fifteen Mk VBs were shipped on *HMS Eagle,* arriving safely on 7th March 1942.

The island had seen one Spitfire previously, an unarmed Photographic Reconnaissance model engaged on missions over Italy. When the first armed Spitfires went into action three days after their arrival they claimed three Luftwaffe aircraft. A hurried retaliation of concentrated attacks on the airfields resulted; Spitfires and Hurricanes were shot up on the ground and these casualties, added to those destroyed and damaged in the air, again left the island practically defenceless. During short periods when it was impossible to send up even one fighter, Control radioed vectoring instructions to imaginary Spitfires while pilots in the control room answered through the same microphone, deluding the monitoring Germans who directed their fighters to empty space. One of the Germans' own fighters was mistakenly shot down as a result of a bogus instruction to non-existent Spitfires.

Two more squadrons, Nos 601 and 603, were sent out from Britain on the

US aircraft carrier *Wasp*. During the voyage, Grumman Wildcat fighters were at readiness on the flight deck as defence and to disguise the mission. The 'tropical' Mk VBs were packed on the hangar deck and some were secured to the ceiling. *Wasp* sailed uneventfully through the Straits of Gibraltar at night and on 20th April, 600 miles from Malta, the Spitfires began to take off, led by the only pilot experienced in deck take-offs – and his plane swung badly, went over the side and was lucky to pick up speed to avoid the 'drink'. The rest got off safely, revving motors with brakes locked on hard, quickly letting go and using up some of the sixty-foot drop to the sea at the end of the run along the flight deck if they had not enough speed to lift their aircraft laden with a ninety-gallon belly tank. Spitfire flap positions were either up or in the ninety-degrees down position which produced too much drag for take-offs. In future carrier deliveries ten degrees of flap were achieved by simply inserting the right thickness of wooden wedges between flap and wing, the wedges being dropped after take-off by fully lowering then lifting the flaps.

On 16th April, in recognition of the valourous stand made by the people of Malta during twenty-two months of almost continuous aerial attack, King George V awarded the George Cross to the island fortress.

Despite the secrecy surrounding the *Wasp's* voyage, German Intelligence discovered that the two squadrons were on the way to Malta and planned an interception over the island. The Spitfires were delayed by flying off course, however, and the Luftwaffe's big reception raid was over when the new arrivals came in to land on the dusty, pitted airfields of Takali and Luqa. While they were off course out over the Mediterranean their leader had asked Malta for a homing course which was quickly given by a German, hoping they would fly his course to Italy. One of the forty-eight Spitfires did not arrive. RAF bombers flying from Malta had sunk so much Axis shipping that two *Fliegerkorps* of fighters and bombers were transferred to the Italian theatre and were based less than a hundred miles away on airfields in Sicily, to take over the attacks on the Malta bases and Allied shipping with which the Italians could not cope. Within a couple of hours of landing at Takali and Luqa, two of the new Spitfires were destroyed and fifteen damaged by Luftwaffe raiders.

On the embattled island, tinned corn beef, dried peas, hard biscuits and olives formed the main diet with a sulphur pill taken after meals to help ward off the raging diarrhoea. Pilots lived under the most trying conditions but were more fortunate than the over-worked ground crews who serviced and repaired aircraft with the same never-flagging devotion as their Battle of Britain comrades, despite the dust, the flies, the shortages of food and water, the bombings and strafings, and the lack of proper hangars in which to work, not to mention the acute shortage of spares. They were as fast as any servicing crews who had to carry fuel in four-gallon cans to get the fighters away again; they were also helped by army and navy personnel who became efficient aircraftsmen. During one attack when fighters had landed to refuel and re-arm, an armourer was seen lying on the wing of a Spitfire, taxiing fast to its take-off position, finishing screwing down a machine gun panel and rolling off just before the pilot opened the throttle.

The Luftwaffe – and the *Regia Aeronautica* which by now had only a minor role – concentrated on the three Malta airfields and anything afloat on Valetta's Grand Harbour, dive-bombing with Ju 87s and Ju 88s, escorted by Me 109s which went on to strafe once the bombs had been dropped. Spotted on radar as they formed up over their Sicilian bases, there was plenty of time for the enemy aircraft to be intercepted out to sea but, with only a few Spitfires to intercept raids of forty to a hundred or more, the enemy always got through – and this happened two or three times a day. Pilots

Above right: Fitters at work on the Malta Spitfires; heat, dust and short rations.
Right: Fuelled and armed, Mk VBs wait for their pilots to sprint out when the next attack develops

'Screwball' Beurling, ace of Malta aces with 33⅓ victories at the end of the war

were rostered for 'readiness' which meant a day spent by the aircraft in blast-proof dispersal bays dispersed along the roads near the airfields. Aircraft flyable but not fighting fit were flown to hide in cloud or far out to sea.

Pilots were alerted by a flare fired from a Verey pistol and those ordered to scramble would taxi their Spitfires to the nearest field and take off with hoods closed against the suffocating dust, taking a little longer than normal to formate because of their wide dispersals, then climb on a vector that usually headed towards the north-east or north-west so that they might attack with the sun behind them. They would dive on the bombers as they came in, with only a little time to fire a burst before the Me 109s claimed their attention. When that fight was over, the Spitfires often had another with Me 109s which attacked aircraft landing and on the ground. This resulted in the development of a special type of Malta landing – one at a time, faster than normal and on paths between craters. The army's anti-aircraft 40mm Bofors guns defended the harbour and airfields and accounted for many Axis aircraft, the gunners' accurate shooting all the more remarkable with barrels badly worn and each gun limited to twelve rounds per day when supplies were short – which was most of the time.

The day after the Spitfires from the *Wasp* landed, more were shot down and shot up on the ground and at the end of the day only eighteen were serviceable. The Spitfires destroyed were not lost cheaply. When pilots fought two or three times a day they quickly became experienced and dangerous – if they managed to survive. As had happened in the Battle of Britain, a few pilots became quick scorers and of these some were outstanding, including Tim Goldsmith, an Australian, 'Screwball' Beurling, a Canadian, and Ray Hesselyn, a New Zealander. On his first two operational flights in one day on Malta, Beurling shot down two Me 109s, a Ju 88, a Ju 87 and probably a Macchi C202. Racing in to intercept three Me 109s bent on jumping a Spitfire as it landed, Beurling got his first Me 109 with a remarkable deflection shot of about sixty degrees, exhibiting the talent of a natural shot that was to take his score to over twenty by the time he was wounded in October.

Apart from the vile living conditions, Malta was a fighter pilot's paradise where those who remained alive and unwounded could add German and Italian crosses to their lists and win decorations and rapid promotion. There were plenty of keen volunteers to go out to the sunny Mediterranean. In May, another batch of Spitfires – sixty-four of them – took off from *Wasp* and *Eagle* which had made the voyage in convoy. Two of the Mk VCs crashed on the island, one tried to alight on the sea when his fuel gave out, one went down on take-off and another pilot established a remarkable feat, after flying back to the carrier when his aircraft's drop-tank had fallen off, by making a dead-stick landing without an arrester hook, without ever having made a deck-landing before. The other fifty-nine

From command of 11 Group in the Battle of Britain to a command in Malta – Sir Keith Park off on a sortie

arrived armed and ready for action except for the need for refuelling. The following day dozens of bombers and fighters attempted to sink an ammunition ship which had run the gauntlet from the Straits but they were matched by as many Spitfires. The Germans lost some forty bombers and fighters that day and the RAF three fighters and one pilot; one Stuka shot down a Spitfire busy shooting down another Stuka. It was not long before No 249 Squadron was the first to reach the century for aircraft downed and their commander, Squadron-Leader Lynch, shot down the 1,000th claimed by the Malta station.

With such strength now existing on Malta, the Germans were forced to terminate this war of attrition to conserve their fighters and bombers for other fronts. The raids continued but they were more sporadic than before. Air-Marshal Park, the successful commander of 11 Group during the Battle of Britain, replaced Air-Marshal Lloyd. Under the new regime, tactics began to change – interceptions were made closer to Sicily and bomb-carrying Spitfires began to drop 250 pounders on Sicilian airfields. When Tobruk was about to fall, Air-Chief-Marshal Tedder asked for Spitfires and Park was able to release No 601 Squadron for service in the Western Desert. Spitfires, assisted by Hurricanes, had won the battle for Malta – an outright victory against superior odds. The commander of the German air forces on Sicily, Kesselring, later paid tribute to the bravery of the RAF's British and Commonwealth pilots who defended the beleagured isle; he was also very impressed with their tactics of diving through the close formations of bombers. The battles for fighter supremacy over Britain and Malta were complete in themselves, where the victor won highly valuable strategic prizes. Malta became a base from where bombers effectively stopped much of the supply of vital equipment for Axis operations in North Africa – control of the Mediterranean had begun to change from the navies to the air forces.

In June and July the desperate air battles over the desert led to fighter shortages in the RAF, worsened to some extent by the presence of the new Me 109Gs. At the beginning of the land battle in the desert, nearly 2,400 sorties were flown by fighters, fighter-bombers and medium bombers during 1st/3rd September. No 145 Squadron had been equipped with Spitfire VBs in May and went into action, flying top cover to Hurricanes, in June. The demand for 'tropical' Spitfires extended beyond the Middle East to India, Ceylon and Australia where Japanese bombers were suddenly within striking distance of cities, ports and military bases. Spitfires were available in Britain but the sea lanes to Egypt, India and Australia were dangerous for transports – particularly in the eastern Indian and Pacific Oceans where Japanese warships could roam virtually at will.

The land actions in the Western Desert were the most important; the British Eighth Army's preparations for the Battle of Alamein which opened on 22nd October, and Operation 'Torch', the Allied landing on French North Africa, on 7th November. With the US Navy emerging victorious in the Pacific, things were beginning to look brighter for the Allies.

Spitfires were flown across from West Africa to provide the Desert Air Force with more Mk VC fighter squadrons which went into top cover over fighter-bombers and medium bombers. After the victory at El Alamein, Rommel's troops retreated, harassed by the Desert Air Force which now included Nos 92, 94 and 417 (RCAF) Spitfire Squadrons. At the other end of the Mediterranean, Seafires of the Royal Navy and Spitfires of Nos 72, 93, 111, 152 and 122 Squadrons RAF together with the 31st and 52nd Fighter Groups USAAF went into action against local fighter opposition and transports over the sea. These Spitfires were flown across from Gibraltar to Algeria. The first American casualties occurred when some French Dewoitine 520 fighters (325 mph, one 20mm cannon, four 7.5mm machine guns) with roundels easily mistaken for British roundels and having a similar appearance to the Hurricane, attacked the Spitfires as they landed, killing one pilot and wounding several others. All but one of the Frenchmen were shot down by a few American fighters which took off after the action began. When General James Doolittle – the ex-Schneider Trophy pilot and leader of the B-25 bomber raid against Tokyo – flew to Algeria, his Flying Fortress was escorted by the American-flown Spitfires.

When Sicily was invaded, Mk Vs were among the support aircraft and the first aircraft to land on the first captured airfield was an out-of-fuel Mk V. At both ends of North Africa, Spitfires were primarily used as top cover escort or defence and Spitfires, clipped locally and fitted with more rounded wooden tip-fairings, were among the ground support aircraft attacking transport columns and Panzers. Fast clipped and cropped Mk VBs were used as reconnaissance aircraft by No 40 Squadron (SAAF). Clipped, bomb-carrying Mk Vs were flown through the Sicilian campaign where their top cover was often a flight of Mk IXs.

Spitfires also served in the Far East in the fight to halt the advance of the Japanese forces towards Australia. In this new theatre, tactics found sufficient against the Germans and Italians were found wanting. The American Volunteer Group flying for Chiang Kai-shek in China had learned the hard way how to fight their P-40s against the more highly manoeuvrable Zeros; the Americans knew that they had no chance in a turning dogfight and that their only hope of success lay in using the superior diving speed of the P-40s to rush down from above, fire a burst at a Zero (Mitsubishi A6M-series) or one of the other very manoeuvrable Japanese radial-engined fighters operating in the China theatre, and then dive away. General Chennault, commanding the AVG, had passed on the results of this operational flying to the authorities in Washington, but

Top right: One of the most inhospitable areas in the world – a Mk V in flight over the Western Desert *Right:* Advance ground crew watch as one of their charges comes in to land at a forward airstrip

the information was either ignored or lost. Thus the quality of Japanese aircraft and pilots came as a great surprise to Allied pilots at the beginning of the Pacific war and the costly process of operational learning had to start again. The information was, however, available when three squadrons of Spitfires arrived in North Australia to relieve an American squadron of P-40 Kittyhawks, defenders of Port Darwin from Japanese fighter and bomber attacks. The Wing was composed of Nos 452 and 457 Squadrons RAAF and No 54 Squadron RAF; their aircraft were Mk VCs.

The two Australian squadrons had been formed in England in April and June, 1941, and saw much of the fighting over the Channel and France – and some of the pilots had fought also at Malta and with the Desert Air Force.

Left: A magnificent air-to-air photograph of a Spitfire VB in flight. Note the blisters for the cannon breeches *Below:* Wing-Commander C R Caldwell (as the markings show) commanding a wing in North Australia

They were recalled at the request of the Australian government when the Japanese expansion reached the islands north of Australia during 1942. Middle East Command had first priority on Spitfires at this time and it was not until early 1943 that the Wing was formed on fighter bases near Darwin. Some of the pilots were experienced, a few with high scores against German and Italian fighters, and the rest were fresh from OTUs. Their leader, Wing-Commander Clive Caldwell, was considered the best fighter commander in the RAAF. The Air Officer Commander-in-Chief RAF Middle East, Air-Chief-Marshal Tedder, said of Caldwell, who had commanded No 112 Squadron RAF: 'a fine commander, an excellent leader and a first-class shot'.

Caldwell's first requirement for a pilot in his wing was good shooting. 'A pilot who could not shoot straight might as well remain on the ground,' he said. Although he commanded some good shots in his Darwin wing their results against the Zeros were were not spectacular. Their man handicaps were that the Japanese bom-

bers were their principal targets, which gave an advantage to escorting fighters, that some pilots were over-keen and neglected to check their fuel gauges, and that the effects of Darwin dust took some of the power from the Merlins, as the sand and dust of the Middle Eastern and North African campaigns did to engines there.

There were several experienced and successful Japanese fighter pilots in the South-West Pacific aea who might successfully attack most Allied pilots, whether they came into range diving, head-on or turning. One of these Japanese aces was attacked from above by two of the most experienced pilots in the USAAF – Tommy Mac-Guire, with a total of thirty-eight victories to his credit at the time of his death, and Major Rittmayer with fourteen. They dived their P-38 Light-nings, one after the other, in their attack on the lone Zero and both Americans were shot down. The Dar-win pilots had plenty of respect for the Zeros but were more than confi-dent that they possessed the superior machine. The Zero had a high power-to-weight ratio, could climb to 10,000 feet in a little over three minutes and could reach 20,000 feet in about the same time as a Mk V Spitfire. The Zero was armed with two cannon and two machine guns, its armour was negligible and the aircraft structure could not take the same punishment as British or American aircraft.

The first Spitfire interception over the Darwin area was made on 6th February 1943, when a Dinah (Mitsu-bishi Ki-46) twin-engined reconnais-sance aircraft was shot down. A few weeks later No 54 Squadron pilots shot down two Zeros and a Kate (Nakajima B5N torpedo bomber). In a big raid on 2nd May, the over-keen Spitfire pilots got into trouble when they intercepted the Japanese bom-bers and fighters on their way home over the Timor Sea. Caldwell had led the wing into the sun and above the raiders, No 54 Squadron attacking

first into the Zero formations where dogfights took place down to 7,000 feet, then the other two squadrons attacked. There was too much dog-fighting against the Zeros, which could turn inside the Spitfires: an Australian who had fought Me 109s over France and who was not only a good shot but also a skilful pilot, made a shallow diving attack on a Zero which performed a tight loop on to the tail of the Spitfire; the Aus-tralian was forced to break quickly to avoid being shot down. Some were shot down and others ran out of fuel and were forced to await rescue in rubber dinghies. Five Spitfires were lost, three pilots were saved, for one Japanese bomber and five fighters. In this action, and others at high alti-tude, freezing caused many cannon to malfunction or jam. If one cannon ceased to function, firing the other swung the aircraft and spoilt the aim.

The Japanese raids were infrequent during the first few months of 1943 and when they did fly over to bomb airfields, barracks and ships in Port Darwin the Spitfires scattered them and accounted for more than they lost. By June, the lack of replace-ments for the quickly wearing Merlins meant that most of the Spitfires had lost much of their power and some were lost in forced-landings in the bush around Darwin. There were two morning raids on 20th June when the wing shot down nine bombers and five fighters, and damaged ten more air-craft for the loss of two Spitfires. In two raids at the end of the month, eight Japanese bombers and six fighters were destroyed; seven Spit-fires were lost, four of these as a result of engine failure. One of the pilots baled out over rough bush country and was dropped food, water and cigarettes until he could be rescued five days later. By July, the Spitfire engines were so worn that in one interception only seven of No 54 Squadron's aircraft reached the Japanese, who lost seven bombers and two fighters out of forty-seven aircraft attacked by the Darwin Wing. That the Japanese aircraft could be superior with a height advantage was demon-strated on 20th August. They had sent over three high-flying reconnaissance aircraft which were shot down near

Top left: Spitfires in Australia, where the dust played havoc with the performance of the engines
Left: Japanese fighter opposition for the Spitfire, the redoubtable Zero, gave the Australians a nasty shock

Spitfire VIIIs on a waterlogged airfield in Burma in the monsoon season

Darwin, then they sent another Dinah in the afternoon and it too was shot down, so they sent yet another, heavily escorted by fighters. No 54 and No 452 Squadrons were scrambled too late to reach a higher altitude than the enemy who shot down three Spitfires for the loss of one confirmed and two probable Japanese fighters. One of the shot down Spitfire pilots, Squadron-Leader Macdonald, was rescued from the bush by Squadron-Leader Fenton, the 'Flying Doctor' of the 1930s, in his Tiger Moth.

The first RAAF Spitfire squadron formed in Australia was No 79, equipped with Mk VCs, which began operations in the South-West Pacific area, based on Kiriwina Island in the Tobriands. At the end of 1943 the Japanese base at Rabaul was being encircled by Allied airfields and the enemy air force was being slowly deci-

mated in the air and on the ground. In this blockade area the Spitfires acted as airfield protection and escorted medium bombers in raids against Rabaul and Japanese barges which moved from island to island, sheltering under camouflaged, low-hanging trees along the banks of river mouths and harbours. The squadron's first kill was a Dinah reconnaissance aircraft, blown up after hits by cannon shells from a distance of 600 yards. Part of a wing also containing two Kittyhawk squadrons, No 77 and No 76 RAAF, the Spitfires moved to Los Negros Island in the Admiralty Group in March 1944. There they flew ground support missions for the US Cavalry invasion forces, strafing while the Kittyhawks operated as fighter-bombers. Led by Wing-Commander Gordon Steege, the Spitfires of No 79 Squadron were the first to fly north

over the Equator. They were also the first to participate in a fishing operation, making a reconnaissance flight for a bomb-carrying Kittyhawk to attack a large school of fish – enough were picked up by the crash-launch to feed the wing!

Mark VCs were in action in Burma for about four months at the end of 1943 before being replaced by Mk VIIIs. When two RAF squadrons received their Mk VCs in September, the British were building up their forces for the offensive which was to sweep the Japanese out of the country. The Spitfires were sent to bolster the Hurricane fighter force which had successfully fought the bombers and fighters of the Japanese Army air force. Based at Alipore, the Spitfires acquitted themselves admirably against the Japanese aircraft – in the first two interceptions two. Dinahs

Above: **Armourers tow a bomb over to a waiting Mk VIII in Burma**
Left: **Line up of 136 Squadron Mk VIIIs on an airstrip in the Cocos Islands**

were downed. In later dogfights some Spitfires were shot down and the squadron learned the hard way how to tackle the manoeuvrable Japanese fighters.

The biggest success was an interception by No 136 Squdron which shot down a flight of Japanese bombers for the loss of one Spitfire whose pilot bailed out. The squadron could claim two Japanese fighters which collided, and a third which crashed when machine-gunning the pilot from the downed Spitfire as he floated down under his parachute.

Spitfire strength and Spitfire pilots

Arduous and prolonged active service had proved the Spitfire to be a reliable aircraft and a successful fighter at all levels though more suited for high altitude work, compared with other British fighters. It had also proved itself very rugged and tough, hundreds of the type surviving the commonest accidents of belly landings and nose-ups; the former was remediable when it was pilot fault, the latter remedied to some degree by the Mk V under-carriage modification. Despite its spindly legs and narrow wheel-track, the aircraft was often flown from rough and uneven fields – particularly on Malta where continuous bombing resulted in a rough surface – and was able to land, though not as success-fully as the sturdy-wheeled Kitty-hawk, on the stone-strewn desert. One of the spectacular desert rescues was one made by Pilot-Officer Terry, an Australian, of a fellow Spitfire pilot whose aircraft had crash-landed near the scene of his strafing; Terry landed beside the other pilot and they took off with the rescued pilot sitting on Terry's knees and handling the con-trol column and throttle while Terry moved the rudder pedals – vengeful Germans arrived on the scene a few minutes later.

The oleo legs took some severe landings in training units and some-times also in squadron service when shot-up pilots or aircraft were lucky to make any sort of landing. Rarely was a landing so heavy that a leg would break or a tyre burst.

Bursting one tyre on landing was not too much of a catastrophe if the pilot knew what to do, and he was able to land on a proper airfield rather than an airstrip where embankments could restrict the ground-loop – the wide, then narrowing swing around the flat-tyred wheel until the speed dropped and the outside wing scraped the ground. Revving up and controlling direction with rudder would keep the aircraft straight while the aircraft had some speed, but when it slowed, braking on the sound wheel could not prevent the inevitable quick ground-loop before stopping. The Momote airstrip on Los Negros Island in the Admiralties was of rolled coral, 5,000

feet long, constructed by US Navy 'Seabees'. There, several Mk VC Spitfires of No 79 Squadron RAAF burst tyres landing or taking-off, the fault not so much the sharp lumps of coral as the poor quality of the tyres manufactured from reclaimed rubber. One pilot made a slow, three-point approach, burst a tyre as soon as the aircraft touched down and swung nose-first into a coral bank before he could increase speed to use rudder control. This time the blowout was caused by a bent corner of pressed steel matting laid over a wet patch at the end of the strip. The tendency for Momote pilots to make fast 'wheelers' – landing tail up – enabled them to keep a steady course if a tyre burst. Ground-loops thrust a heavy load on oleo legs, but these proved they could take the strain.

For short-term expediency many modifications were carried out on stations, and sometimes Spitfires were sent into battle wearing parts quite foreign to them. During the Battle of Britain, the wing of one Spitfire was temporarily patched with thin tinplate from a four-gallon fuel drum and a holed wing-root on one Spitfire was patched with a piece of cockpit armour plating. The activities of the innovators and modifiers at the RAAF's No 103 Maintenance Unit at Aboukir in Egypt would have surprised the engineers back home at the Supermarine works: the development of desert HF machines from Mk Vs, to catch Ju 86P reconnaissance aircraft flying unmolested at 40,000 feet over Egyptian bases, was a successful accomplishment already mentioned. Rudder bars were cut down, engines souped up, lightweight batteries installed, four-blade airscrews fitted, armour plate removed, carburettors modified, wingtips elongated and armament reduced to two 0.5-inch machine guns. Three test pilots from the Aboukir depot suffered severe pain, partial paralysis and blackouts flying these unpressurised machines at heights up to 50,000 feet, but Flying-Officer Reynolds, Pilot-Officers Gold and Genders put an end to the enemy's photographic missions. Aboukir-designed filters were another local success and another variation was the moving of cannon from the inboard to outboard position in some Mk VCs.

At Hornchurch the sturdiness and sometimes the safety of an upturned Spitfire was demonstrated when one skidded a hundred yards upside down and the pilot suffered only a minor head wound; this Spitfire had been taking off to attack marauding bandits when one of them dropped a bomb underneath it. When a pilot undid his seat straps in an upside down Spitfire he was careful to brace himself so that he did not drop on his head. The small side flap beneath the hood on the port side of the fuselage allowed him to crawl out or be pulled out in case of fire, the biggest danger in minor crashes.

Landing undercarriage-up on smooth strips or fields never hurt pilots unless the approach was made lop-sided. A few pilots inadvertently attempted to fly with propeller-pitch at fully coarse and sank lower and lower as the Spitfire lost altitude and, in endeavours to hold them over tree tops, stalled, crashing down from twenty or thirty feet at a little over 70 mph. If the ground were flat and free from obstacles in the few yards needed for the 'landing', the pilots walked away uninjured. 'It's a good landing if you can walk away from it' was one of the comic expressions heard on training stations. One Spitfire, shot down at low level near Millingimbi, crashed along the ground, somersaulting and skidding while it lost both wings and most of its tail, yet the pilot was able to 'walk away'. Being tightly strapped in by the safety harness saved many lives and prevented serious injuries.

Crashing in the air, too, happened often in combat from deliberate ramming or accidental colliding, and the latter also happened in training. As long as there was no fire or explosion and as long as the pilots were not physically restricted, the tough construction around the Spitfire's cockpit allowed many pilots to climb out and parachute to safety.

In the tropics and North Africa, Spitfire pilots usually taxied their planes with the cockpit side flap down, because of the heat, and occasionally someone would forget and take off with the 'door' open; it could, of course, be easily closed in flight. Those who forgot and had thought they had closed the flap could always blame 'gremlins', a kind of atmospheric little folk who interfered with ailerons, booted the rudder, blocked the carburettor, coarsened the pitch and fiddled with things they knew absolutely nothing about, with a greater penchant for bombers than fighters.

With gremlins about, as well as the enemy and careless pilots, Spitfire toughness saved many lives. Some Spitfires landed with wings forced up into a more pronounced dihedral from being pulled too steeply out of dives at over 500 mph; they landed with rudders shot to pieces, with the upper surface of a wing crumpled and an aileron missing after a near-miss by an exploding shell, with jammed trimmers, with cockpits in shambles, with a magneto destroyed and a couple of cylinders out of action, with large holes in the fuselage or tail or a few feet of wing tip shot off. The most remarkable flying Spitfire was one which struggled back from the Channel with some of one wing missing, holes in the other and in the fuselage and elevators, part of the tail torn away and the pilot wounded; it barely scraped over a coastal cliff, smashed more than a foot from the blades of the propeller on a stone wall and managed to fly on to belly-land in a farmer's field.

Wing-Commander B E 'Paddy' Finucane, DSO, DFC, wrote these impressions of some of his experiences as a fighter pilot:

'Before going on a trip I usually have a funny feeling in my tummy, but once I'm in my aircraft everything is fine. The brain is working fast, and if the enemy is met it seems to work like a clockwork motor. Accepting that, rejecting that, sizing up this, and remembering that. You don't have time to feel anything. But your nerves may be on edge – not from fear, but from excitement and the intensity of the mental effort. I have

Right: 'Paddy' Finucane, fifth on the list of RAF aces with thirty-two victories at the time of his death

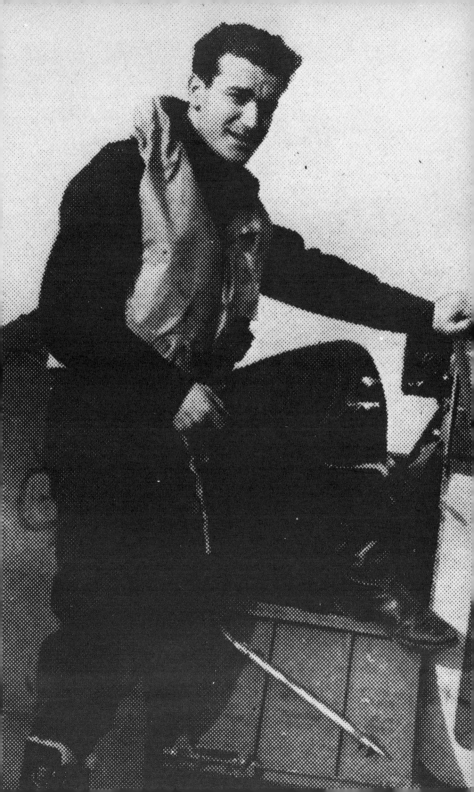

come back from a sweep to find my tunic wet through with perspiration.

'Our chaps sometimes find that they can't sleep. What happens is this. You come back from a show and find it very hard to remember what happened. Maybe you have a clear impression of three or four incidents, which stand out like illuminated lantern slides in the mind's eyes. Perhaps a picture of two Me 109s belting down on your tail from out of the sun and already within firing range. Perhaps another picture of your cannon shells striking at the belly of an Me and the aircraft spraying debris around. But for the life of you, you can't remember what you did. Later, when you have turned in and sleep is stealing over you, some tiny link in the chain of events comes back. Instantly you are fully awake, and then the whole story of the operation pieces itself together and you lie there, sleep driven away, re-living the combat, congratulating yourself for this thing, blaming yourself for that. The reason for this is simply that everything happens so quickly in the air that you crowd a tremendous amount of thinking, action and emotion into a very short space of time, and you suffer afterwards from mental indigestion.

'The tactical side of the game is quite fascinating. You get to learn, for instance, how to fly so that all the time you have a view behind you as well as in front. The first necessity in combat is to see the other chap before he sees you, or at least before he gets the tactical advantage of you. The second is to hit him when you fire. You mightn't have a second chance.'

Finucane was a regular air force officer, born in Dublin. He was killed in action in July 1942, at the age of twenty-one.

Britain's most experienced young airmen in 1939 were her regular officers and NCOs. Thorough and intensive training at the RAF Cadet College at Cranwell produced pilots who could fly immaculate formations and aerobatics, and at the Central Flying School refinements of instruction were developed which became standards for instructors at other flying schools. As well as the regulars, there were the Volunteer Reserve, composed of men of eighteen or nineteen engaged on a short service commission for five years, the Auxiliary Air Force and the university air squadrons, all widening the scope for recruiting pilots. Commissions for short service attracted young men from all over the Empire; more than a hundred New Zealanders, Australians, Canadians and South Africans, wearing the sky-blue uniform of the RAF, fought in the Battle of Britain.

Total numbers of officers and men in the RAF increased from 55,000 in 1937 to 118,000 in 1939, when over 5,000 volunteer reservists were serving or in training as air crew. An ambitious plan to train thousands more was the establishment of the Empire Air Training Scheme (EATS) for which an agreement was signed by the various countries at Ottawa on 17th December 1939.

The Women's Auxiliary Air Force was formed in June that year and WAAFs served in all branches of the service – except as air crew. The only WAAF known to make a Spitfire flight was a girl who made the flight hanging on to the tail structure. It happened on 9th February 1945, at Hibalston, when Flight-Lieutenant Cox ran up his engine with several 'erks', including Leading Aircraftswoman Margaret Horton, sitting on and leaning over the tail. Cox throttled back, then opened the throttle up again too soon and took off before LACW Horton had time to drop off. Up she went, her body across the tail and one hand pressed against an elevator, with the pilot complaining to the control tower duty officer that the Spitfire was behaving strangely. Control recalled him but did not mention the WAAF, in case he panicked. Cox landed, stopped at the end of his run where Margaret Horton dropped off, tested his controls without knowing that she had been on the tail, and took off again. 'Put yourself down for ten minutes flying time,' he told her later.

Pilots who flew fighters were flamboyant members of the service, expressing their individuality and raising official eyebrows when they 'carried on' if there was the slightest relaxation in official restrictions. In isolated areas, in the desert, Burma or the South-West Pacific, completely unorthodox clothing replaced some items of normal service-issue uniforms; the outstanding example being, it is said, a fighter pilot who used to wear his hunting pink and breeches while jeep-chasing the desert fox and once had to wear this rig in his fighter when he was scrambled before he had time to change. Most grew moustaches at one time or another and groups were observed on a Pacific island, combing out and comparing their lip tresses as they sipped canned American beer in the tropical evenings. As in other wars, moustaches were associated with a particular service; there were Guards moustaches, Cavalry moustaches and the waxed, twirled-end variety favoured by sergeant-majors from the days of the Boer War to the present time. In the British and Commonwealth air forces in the Second World War, wide, brushed up moustaches became known as Spitfire moustaches, a tribute to

The Duke of Kent, Air Commodore in the Welfare Branch, killed in an air accident in August 1942

their best fighter and possibly because the name sounded better than, say, Kittyhawk, Hurricane, Mosquito or Typhoon moustache. They particularly suited the dress of corduroy trousers, suede boots, bright scarves and battered caps of the 'elegant' desert pilots. Pilots who flew their Spitfires from Darwin to Perth during an emergency in 1943 arrived 'scarlet-eyed, bearded, sunburned and unkempt'.

The Duke of Kent, the Duke of Windsor's youngest brother, gave up his post at the Admiralty and transferred to the RAF with the rank of Air-Commodore in the Welfare Branch, a position which entailed visiting many air force stations. On one of these visits, a semi-official inspection, he met a group of fighter pilots with the top button of his tunic inadvertently undone. The pilots of that squadron adopted the popular Duke's three-done-up-one-undone fashion as a style for themselves and were in turn imitated by fighter pilots in other squadrons, a sartorial quirk tolerated by most commanders – except when on the parade ground. The

Indistinguishable from their RAF comrades – the pilots of a Belgian Spitfire squadron

Duke was killed in an aircraft accident in Scotland while flying from Invergordon to Iceland in August 1942.

Richard Hillary was a University Air Squadron pilot, representative perhaps of the Oxford generation which went to war on 3rd September 1939. His opinions of himself and his friends are described in his book *The Last Enemy*:

'We were disillusioned and spoiled. The press referred to us as the Lost Generation and we were not displeased. Superficially we were selfish and egocentric without any Holy Grail in which we could lose ourselves. The war provided it, and in a delightfully palatable form. It demanded no heroics, but gave us the opportunity to demonstrate in action our dislike of organised emotion and patriotism, the opportunity to prove to ourselves and to the world that our effete veneer was not as deep as our dislike of interference, the opportunity to prove that, undisciplined though we might be, we were a match for Hitler's dogma-fed youth.'

A keen University oarsman, Hillary had gone on an organised tour in 1938. Rowing in a leaky boat against a German crew for the Göring Fours Prize, the Englishmen were described by a sneering German oarsman as 'thoroughly representative of a decadent race' when their attitude to the row appeared casual and lackadaisical. The Germans were sullen and resentful when the British crew won.

Hillary's fellow sergeant-volunteers were representatives of every class and calling who rushed to the Volunteer Reserve Centre the day war was declared. A year later, Pilot-Officer Hillary was flying his Spitfire in No 603 Squadron based at Hornchurch. He had had trouble with a new canopy sticking in its grooves and, as was his habit, flew without gloves and with his goggles up on his forehead. The squadron found a gaggle of Me 109s, one of which Hillary attacked from 200 yards, from slightly to one side, and observed strikes from his deflection shooting. Then, instead of breaking or making sure his own tail was clear, he fired again until the Messerschmitt flamed and spiralled away – just as his own aircraft was hit and set aflame. By the time he got his sticking canopy open his cockpit was a mass of flame. Eventually, he fell out unconscious, was revived in the cold air, pulled his ripcord and fell, badly burned on hands and face, into the sea. Over a period of many months his burns and scars were slowly, painfully repaired by the brilliant skin surgeon from New Zealand, Dr McIndoe. Hillary went back to flying but was killed during a night-flying exercise from an OTU.

Pilots were instructed when they joined their squadrons that it would be bad form to discuss women or 'shop' in the mess and that the regulars used to prefer local pubs for that kind of talk. Pilots discovered on joining their squadrons that there was scarcely any conversation that did not include women or flying, mostly flying: it was easier to 'open the hangar doors' over a beer than to interest their fellows in other subjects. Besides, there was so much for the newcomers to learn and so much for the old hands to recount. A senior commander described the pilots of Fighter Command as a flamboyant, reckless, harum-scarum happy band of playboys, gallant and courageous when the heat was on; an apt description of the majority.

Some battle-experienced types adopted attitudes of languid arrogance, cynical about red tape and stiff parade ground manners. Tales of death were couched in jolly euphemisms – 'old so-and-so bought it – pranged into the scenery with his kite shot to pieces; and his number-two went for a Burton on the way back' – attitudes and expressions rooky pilots soon learned to imitate. They also learned the traditional RAF songs and the bawdier compositions of the mysteriously anonymous. *The Bold Aviator* (or *The Dying Airman*) was inherited from the earlier war when pilots sang, it seemed, grouped around a candle-lit piano, drinking champagne:

'Oh, the bold aviator was dying,
 And as 'neath the wreckage he lay,
   he lay,

Top right: Spitfire pilots wait (in the sun) for their next sortie
Right: Pilots discuss the route to be flown with the commanding officer

Left: Final briefing from her CO as an ATA pilot climbs into her Spitfire for a ferry flight

To the sobbing mechanics about him
These last parting words he did say:
Take the cylinders out of my kidneys
The connecting rod out of my brain,
    my brain,
From the small of my back get the
    camshaft
And assemble the en-gyne again.'
    Verses were added and changed in
both wars. The old songs were not
considered by the new generation to
be as terrific as *O'Riley's Daughter,
Lydia Pink, The Ball of Kerriemuir,
Bang Away Lulu,* and *Cats on the
Rooftops.* Out in the Pacific, RAF pilot
behaviourisms were perpetuated and
new songs like *Send Her Down* and *An
Airman Lay Dying on Papuan Soil*
bewildered eavesdropping Melanes-
ians. The choruses swelled at parties,
the instant parties to celebrate new
arrivals, time-expired departees, victories and deaths; parties that were
wildly uninhibited and exuberant,

and likely to end with a wrestling, wrecking football match with perhaps a visitor's cap, preferably gold-braided, used as the ball. A general consensus of opinion was that British parties were the best there were: their capacity for departing from a natural reserve and letting go at a party was astoundingly enormous. Wise commanders kept flying to a minimum after a mess 'do' when judgements in the air were likely to be somewhat awry. Wise pilots kept as physically fit as conditions allowed.

Some nicknames were attached at birth and others were handed out in squadron service; many are now permanently registered in the histories: 'Sailor' Malan, 'Tin Legs' Bader, 'Killer' Caldwell, 'Bluey' Truscott, 'Cobber' Kane, 'Scruffy' Makin, 'Black Jack' Walker, 'Cowboy' Blatchford, 'Rasp' Berry, 'Gilli' Wright and 'Dusty' for members of the Rhodes family. Heavily braided gents of the upper echelons had borne theirs from youthful re-christenings: 'Boom' Trenchard, 'Stuffy' Dowding, 'Dingbat' Saunders, 'Zulu' Morris, 'Daddy' Nichols and 'Bum and Eyeglass' Higgins, to name a few

Early in the war the majority of fighter pilots in the RAF were Britons; in the Battle of Britain they formed eighty per cent of the force and the rest were from the Commonwealth – Australians, Canadians, New Zealanders, South Africans, Rhodesians, Indians – and from Poland, France, Czechoslovakia, Norway, Denmark, Holland, Belgium, Ireland – some Irishmen joined as British nationals while others remained Irish – and from neutral America. As more and more pilots from the occupied countries and trained or partly-trained airmen from the EATS centres arrived, the proportion of non-Britons rose. Several Spitfire squadrons were eventually almost entirely composed of non-Britons; there were enough Australian fighter pilots, for example, serving in RAF squadrons to form several wings, but for the duration of the war most of them remained scattered.

Spitfire pilots were of all sorts, from all kinds of backgrounds, with good co-ordination and eyesight and some aggression and common sense as common denominators. Physically, some were short (only one was as short as American 'Shorty' Keogh's four feet and ten inches), many were over six feet tall and the average was about five feet and nine inches. Size had little to do with fighter ability; flying skill, good shooting and awareness were the prime essentials.

The tail-gripping Margaret Horton was not the only woman who became airborne with a Spitfire. Before D-Day in 1944, two new Spitfires landed and taxied up to the tarmac of a fighter station where a group of pilots admired the perfect three-pointers. When the pilots stepped out of the cockpits and removed their helmets, the watching air force men were astounded to see that one of the pilots was a beautiful blonde girl and the other a middle-aged, one-armed man! Blondes and one-armed men flying Spitfires! *Civilians* flying Spitfires! These improbable pilots were Joan Dutton and Stewart Keith-Jopp, and they were not quite civilians, being members of the Air Transport Auxiliary. The ATA was formed in 1939 by Gerard d'Erlanger, who was appointed Commodore, to assist the air force in ferrying aircraft from factories to the stations. Experienced men like Keith-Jopp (who also only had one eye) had flown in the first war and others had many hours of flying time on civilian aircraft. By the end of the war hundreds of ATA pilots, including women who were first recruited in 1940 by Miss Pauline Gower, had delivered thousands of military aircraft, from Tiger Moths to Stirling four-engined bombers; in 1944 they delivered 10,000 four-engined bombers, many of them across the Atlantic, and early that year *girls* delivered as many as twenty Spitfires, Tempests and Typhoons a day to forward airfields on the south-eastern areas of England. At the age of twenty-two, Joan Hughes had 600 hours flying time and ferried Stirlings, among other types. Lettice Curtis delivered over 150 Mosquitoes and 400 heavy bombers. Men and women from twenty-eight countries were represented among the flying staff of ATA and some of them were qualified to fly 134 different types of aircraft. To them, the Spitfire was a piece of cake.

Marks VI-XI

Flexibility in the Spitfire design was cleverly engineered, and changes from mark to mark were made easily on the production lines or in service; for example, an order for Mk VBs placed at Supermarine, Castle Brômwich or Westland could be altered to Mk VCs, Mk IXs or Seafire IIBs. By 1941, the fighter was made to order for a variety of roles and all, except those with Vokes filters, clipped or extended wings, looked much the same. The wing span was to remain constant, except for clipped and extended models, at 36 feet 10 inches right through to the F 22. Lengths varied, 29 feet 11 inches in the Marks I–III and V to 32 feet 11 inches in the F 22, with intermediate marks having lengths somewhere between these two limits depending on the engine fitted and the chord of the fin and rudder.

The first Mk VI was built as a prototype for high-flying Spitfires, with wings extended to 40 feet 2 inches, their area to 248.5 square feet, and fuselage length to 30 feet 2¼ inches. Merlin 47s of 1,415 hp were fitted to the one hundred production models, together with a pressure cabin and its supercharger, these giving the Mk VI a service ceiling of 40,000 feet and a maximum speed of 364 mph at 22,000 feet. This was the first production model to use the four-blade Jablo Rotol airscrew. Of the one hundred production models most were fitted with the 'B' wing and a few with the 'A' wing. Extensions to the wings improved controllability at the high altitudes where the German high-altitude bombers and reconnaissance aircraft were hunted. Work on a pressurised cabin had begun as early as 1940 at the Royal Aircraft Establishment at Farnborough and also at Supermarine and, after testing in a Mk V in 1941, it was ready for fitting to the HF VI production types in 1942, when Nos 117, 124, 521, 602 and 616 Squadrons flew them. The pressurised cockpit cabin was fitted with a canopy screwed down from outside to seal in the air; the access-flap was removed and replaced with continuous fuselage construction. The Marshall cabin

Left: Spitfire VI, the first production model with a pressurised cockpit and a special high altitude engine

blower gave a 28,000 feet apparent pressure at 40,000 feet. At this height the aircraft lost some of its longitudinal stability. Another flying characteristic, which was felt at high speeds, was a heaviness of stick controls. Mk VIs served in Europe, though a few found their way to the Middle East.

The first marked change in the Spitfire came with the next mark, the Mk VII – over a foot longer, with a retractable tailwheel (first adopted in the Mk III), a 1,565 hp Merlin 61 or 64, of 1,710 hp, six instead of three exhaust ports on each side and, in later models, a more pointed and broader-chord rudder which also made for a better balance in design. The greatest departure from previous Spitfire models was, however, in the loss of the characteristic asymmetrical cooling system protuberances under the wings. The redesign had done away with this feature and replaced it with symmetrical housings for the supercharger intercooler and the oil cooler. Both normal and extended 'C' wings were fitted to variants of the Mk VII, all of which were 'F' models except for sixteen 'HF' models fitted with the high-altitude Merlin 71 of 1,475 hp.

The prototype Mk VII was built on a Mk V airframe, strengthened for the Merlin 60 series which weighed 1,630-plus pounds, over 200 pounds heavier than the previous series used in Spitfires. These Merlins were built with a two-stage supercharger with an intercooler; the second stage of the blower came in at a predetermined height and was controlled either automatically to come in at that height, or was switched over manually after the height was reached. In formation flying the practice was for the leader to co-ordinate a manual change-over to maintain good formation otherwise made ragged as individual aircraft shot forward until checked as their blowers came in: if all second-stage blowers were set for 18,000 feet, they would come in automatically within about one hundred feet of the height but no two aircraft blowers came in together at the same instant. When the second stage did come in there was a glorious thump at the pilot's back as the extra power pulled the aircraft suddenly forward.

The general performance was higher than that of the Mk VI. The HF's new double-glazed hood could be slid back or jettisoned for emergency exits. The extended 'C' wings were modified to carry a fourteen gallon fuel tank in each, the fuel from these tanks being pumped into the main fuselage tank, by throwing a switch in the cockpit, when there was room for it; combat range was increased 150 miles beyond the 510 mile range of the Mk VI. The four-blade Rotol and the extra length of the nose gave a total height of 12 feet 7¼ inches to the top of the vertical airscrew. With a Merlin 64, maximum speed rose to 408 mph at 25,000 feet, 382 mph at 12,500 feet and maximum cruising speed was 324 mph at 20,000 feet. It could climb to 20,000 feet no faster than the Mk II but could reach 43,000 feet and still operate usefully as a fighter. 140 were built, serving in ten squadrons in Europe and the Middle East.

Pierre Clostermann described an interception made by Mk VIIs in his book *The Big Show*:

' "Hallo, Dalmat Red one, Pandor calling, bandit approaching B for Baker, at angels Z for Zebra, climb flat on vector zero, nine, five. Out!"

'I fumbled inside my boot for my code card, which had got mixed up with my maps. I was so clumsy about it I had to ask Pandor to repeat.

'O.K. a Jerry was approaching Scapa Flow, at altitude Z – I looked it up on the card. Phew! Z meant 40,000 feet. I set my course, still climbing at full boost. Ian's Spit hovered a few yards away . . . the arctic sun pierced my eyeballs. I switched on the heating and set the pressure in my cabin . . . In five minutes we had got to 23,000 feet.

'Forty-one thousand feet! The cold was really getting frightful and I turned the oxygen full on. Thanks to the pressurised cockpit the pain was bearable. From now on our exhaust gases left a heavy white trail which stretched out and widened behind us like the wake of a ship. We had the sun behind us.

'Our special engines were pulling beautifully and our lengthened wing supported us well in the rarefied air. Ian was parallel to me, about 900

yards away, and we had gained about another 2,000 feet, which brought us roughly 1,000 feet higher than our quarry, who was about two miles away and approaching rapidly. He must be as blind as a bat.

' "Tally-ho, Ian, ready to attack?"

' "O.K."

'He had seen us, but too late. We converged on him. To our surprise it was a Messerschmitt 109G equipped with two fat auxiliary tanks under the wings. He shone like a newly minted penny and he was camouflaged pale-grey above and sky-blue underneath. He had no nationality marks.

'First he turned left, but Ian was there, veering towards him. He reversed his turn, saw me, and, with a graceful continuous movement, banked more steeply, rolled gently over on his back, diving vertically in the hope of leaving us behind.

'Without hesitation we followed him. He dived straight towards the grey sea which looked congealed, without a wrinkle. He was half a mile ahead of us, with his tanks still fixed to his wings. The speed increased dizzily. At these heights, you have to be careful because you soon reach the speed of sound and then, look out! There is a strong risk of finding yourself hanging on a parachute, in your underpants, in less time than it takes to describe it.

'. . . At 27,000 feet my AS indicator showed 440 mph, that is a true speed of 600 mph! I had both hands on the stick and I leant on the controls with all my strength to keep the aircraft in a straight line. The slightest swerve could have crumpled up the wings. I felt my Spitfire jumping all the same, and I could see the paint cracking on the wings, while the engine was beginning to race.

'The controls were jammed. We still went on down – 15,000 feet.: Ian passed me; 10,000 feet: Ian was 200 yards ahead and 600 from the Hun. He opened fire – just a short burst.

'The Me 109G suddenly tore in half like tissue paper, and exploded like a grenade.'

Clostermann used the elevator trim to help him pull the aircraft out of its power-dive, but blacked-out in the process.

'When I opened my eyes again the

headlong momentum had carried me up to 13,000 feet. There was a warm trickle from my nostrils, dripping on to my silk gloves – blood . . . I was alone in the sky, I couldn't see Ian anywhere. Down below, a large iridescent patch of oil and petrol and a puff of smoke wafted away by the wind showed the grave of the Messerschmitt.'

Ian's aircraft had been damaged by the debris from the Me, had made a belly landing on Stronsay and he was brought back from the island 'frozen to the marrow but as happy as a sandboy'.

The Merlin 60 series began with the 60 and 61, both with a reduction gear of .42 to 1. Those of the series used in Spitfires were these and also the 63 with a modified supercharger drive and a horse-power of 1,650; the further modified 63A of 1,710 hp; the 64 of 1,710 hp, which was a 61 with Marshall supercharging for cabin pressurisation; the 66 of 1,580 hp, and the 70 and 71, which were of 1,475 hp and had different supercharger ratios to the 66; the 71 was connected with a cabin supercharger and the 77 was of the same horse power. Finally, the 266 was a 66 built under licence by the Packard motor car company in America. Although the more powerful Rolls-Royce Griffon powered Spitfires from the Mk XII on (except for experiments), Packard Merlins were installed in Spitfire XVIs.

Two squadrons of HF VIs were top cover during the Dieppe raid in August 1942. There were also some IXs but the forty-two squadrons of Mk Vs were responsible for most of the thirty German bombers and fighters shot down; eighty-eight Spitfires were lost and most of the pilots who managed to bale out were taken prisoner: the Mk V was becoming obsolete. The Dieppe raid proved again the importance of keeping up with the Germans in the race to build better and faster aircraft. It was therefore necessary to incorporate improvements on the Mk Vs on the production lines. This resulted in the Mk IX, which was meant to be an interim fighter until the Mk VIII had been developed to a more efficient and more aerodynamically sound frame for the higher powered Merlins intended for this Mark.

The Mk VIII developed as a true individual type rather than an interim stop-gap fighter. The bulk of the production Mk VIIIs, which first went into squadron service in August 1943, were LF versions – their maximum speed with Merlin 66s was attained at 21,000 feet while the F and HF versions with Merlin 61s, 63s and 70s attained their maximum speeds at 25,000 feet. These speeds were 404 mph (LF), 408 mph (F) and 416 mph (HF). As in the Mk VII, the tailwheel was retractable and the wing was the universal 'C' with fourteen-gallon tanks built in.

Of the 1,658 built, only 160 were HF, 267 were F and the rest were LF. The Vokes Aero Vee tropical filter was built in as standard – but fitted in a less obtrusive housing than the filters on the Mk V, and thus the new Spitfire was more suited for service overseas. (They were shipped to the Middle East air force and first went into service with No 145 Squadron in Italy; No 155 Squadron flew them in action with the Red Army forces in the Russian theatre before operating over Burma, in December 1943, with other Mk VIII squadrons; No 253 Squadron flew them in the Allies' Balkan Air Force; and about 400 were shipped to Australia where they were just too late to find more than about a score of Japanese aircraft to test the capabilities of the Mk VIII – and most of these were the ubiquitous Dinah.) Armour was increased to 202 pounds, modifications were incorporated for one 500-pound or two 250-pound bombs and a maximum range of 660 miles on internal fuel was increased to 1,180 miles with drop tanks holding 170 gallons. The lower-powered (1,475 hp) Merlin 70 in the HF version had a different supercharger ratio for packing in the thin air of the sub-stratosphere. As mentioned above the redesigning of the cooling system for the 60-series engines provided an enlarged air intake under the port wing and at last the head-on view of the Spitfire's underneath section was symmetrical in the Mk VII and succeeding marks.

By the time the Mk VIIIs arrived in Australia, and were allowed to languish at Aircraft Depots while modifications were slowly effected and tyres perished in the heat. The air war in the South-West Pacific was monopolised by the US Fifth Air Force, while the RAAF was employed covering the ground forces employed on wasteful mopping-up operations in Borneo and Dutch New Guinea and at Bougainville and Rabaul. Clive Caldwell, now a Group-Captain, led the RAAF Spitfire wing comprising Nos 79, 452 and 457 Squadrons on bombing and strafing missions against sea transports, airfields and enemy ground forces. Targets were sometimes hard to locate and Spitfires flew low over jungles, to draw Japanese fire and thus discover their gun positions. By this time in the war the Japanese took few prisoners and executed shot-down pilots as a matter of course. The Philippines and Okinawa had been invaded, and Japan's fate was sealed: it was astoundingly foolish of the Australian government to waste unnecessarily the lives of airmen and soldiers in Borneo or anywhere else south of Saipan.

In February and March 1945, much of the annual 150 inches of rain fell on the First Tactical Air Force base at Moratai in the Halmahera group of islands east of Borneo, south of the Philippines and west of Dutch New Guinea. The South-West Pacific area was really no place for single-engined aircraft though it was ideal for Beaufighters, which could carry a heavy armament over long distances and could return safely if one motor gave out. When Group-Captains Caldwell and Arthur, Wing-Commanders Gibbes and Ranger, and Squadron-Leaders Waddy, Grace, Vanderfield and Harpham tendered their resignations as a protest against the government's wasteful policy, the fussy political result was an enquiry before a commissioner and the fact that spirits and beer had been sold by Australian servicemen to Americans was made a big and vulgar issue and more or less camouflaged the serious complaints made by the commanders. General MacArthur, the supreme commander in the South-West Pacific Area said in reference to the by-passed areas, 'the actual time of their destruction is of little or no importance'. The Japanese themselves wondered why

the Australian forces bothered to carry on operations against them.

There was better and more realistic hunting for interceptors in Burma; the Japanese not only had some fighters left, there were a few outstanding new fighters, such as the Mitsubishi J2M *Raiden* (Jack), on which to test the Mk VIII's abilities. In one violent tropical thunderstorm, No 615 Squadron lost eight of its sixteen Spitfires, four crashing and four being abandoned in the air. The formation broke up when strong up and down draughts flung the small fighters thousands of feet up or down, turning, skidding and rocking uncontrollably with the control column threshing around in the cockpit as a result of the immense forces working on the ailerons and elevators.

By December 1944, the British Fourteenth Army was back across the Chindwin river and established on the Burma plain. Nine squadrons of Mk VIIIs, including one PR squadron, were among the thirty-one fighter squadrons employed in defence, interception of bombers and reconnaissance aircraft, escort for bombers and fighter-bombers (the Hurricanes and Kittyhawks were the real workhorses) and support of ground troops with strafing and bombing. The inevitable Dinahs were intercepted with ease by the new Spitfires although one did give trouble. Flying-Officer R E J MacDonald of No 152 Squadron was engaged in shooting down a Dinah when it discharged from its tail a missile which exploded and made small holes in the nose and wing of the Spitfire. The best individual shooting occurred when two Spitfires were sent to intercept one enemy aircraft which turned out to be six, then twenty, and finally over forty. Notwithstanding the odds, Flying-Officer G W Andrews and Flight-Sergeant H B Chatfield attacked and got at least three bombers and a fighter. On New Year's Eve one Spitfire was lost and the pilot saved when No 136 Squadron shot down eight bombers and three fighters.

At this stage of the war the Fleet Air Arm was at times in close contact with the Japanese, flying Seafires over wide areas of ocean to hit airfields on Japanese home and outlying islands.

Vickers Supermarine LF IXE (129 Squadron, April 1946)
Engine: Rolls-Royce Merlin 66, 1,720 hp *Armament:* Two 20mm Hispano
Mk II cannon with 120 rounds per gun and two .5-inch Browning machine-guns
with 250 rounds per gun, plus one 500 lb and two 250 lb bombs
Maximum speed: 408 mph at 25,000 feet *Initial climb rate:* 4,100 feet per
minute *Ceiling:* 43,000 feet *Range:* 434 miles normal, 980 miles max
Weight empty: 5,800 lbs *Weight loaded:* 7,500 lbs *Span:* 32 feet 2 inches
Length: 31 feet 0½ inch

Improved Daimler-Benz, BMW and Junkers Jumo engines provided the motive power that gave the Me 109s and Fw 190s a lead in the race for speed and climb, until the Merlin 60 series engines were delivered from Rolls-Royce factories to power the faster Spitfire Mk IXs.

The Mk V production lines were stopped and conversions to Mk IXs began with little time lost in the process; there was no need for a prototype as this Spitfire was another successful make-shift interim model. In July 1942, the first IXs went to No 64 Squadron and by the time the Allies landed in Normandy in June 1944, thousands of the new mark had been delivered to the RAF and over a thousand shipped to the Russian air force. Altogether, 5,665 Mk IXs were built: 4,010 LF, 1,255 F and 400 HF, with the same Merlin range as used in the Mk VIII. Production began on Mk IX frames with stiffened rear fuselages and strengthened engine mountings. Most of the wings were 'C' type, some were 'B' and others the new 'E' wing which was built to carry two cannon and two 0.50 inch Browning heavy machine guns, the cannon and gun mountings being close together in each wing. Racks for two 250 pound bombs were also fitted as standard equipment on the 'E' wing.

It is interesting to compare the general performance of the similarly engined Mk VIIIs and Mk IXs, the one developed from a prototype and the other from a converted Mk V. They looked similar but the Mk IX looked more like a Mk V with its fixed tailwheel. Both had the same weight of armour, they weighed 5,800 pounds empty, but the Mk IXs' loaded weight was 7,500 pounds while that of the Mk VIIIs was 7,767 pounds, the overload weights being respectively 9,000 pounds and 8,000 pounds. Their maximum speeds were the same but the range for the Mk IX was only 434 miles, as it did not have the two fourteen gallon tanks that were built into the Mk VIII's universal wings. Both could climb to 20,000 feet in about six and a half minutes and, fitted with the 'E' wing, the Mk IX had a slightly higher service ceiling. The main advantage of the Mk VIII was that it was more suitable for dusty and tropical conditions.

At first, the similar appearance of the Mk IX to the Mk VB and Mk IIB gave it a tactical advantage when clashing with Me 109s and Fw 190s – until the enemy accepted the fact that all Spitfires might be Mk IXs and worthy of wary respect. This advantage gained from the similarity to the older types brought spectacular results in North Africa when half a dozen Mk IXs, flown by experienced pilots and led by a famous Polish fighter pilot named Salski, joined the Mk Vs that were already winning the battle for fighter supremacy over the 109s and 190s in Tunisia. The Spitfires, with Salski's group predominant, shot down thirty-eight enemy aircraft in one day in the spring of 1943. In the

same theatre, radar and fast interception by the Allied fighters ended the flights of the huge Me 323s and the Ju 52/3M transports carrying the last supplies to the Axis forces. The British and American armies captured Bizerta on 7th May 1943; on 3rd September they landed in the toe of Italy after having captured Sicily. More Mk IXs covered and supported these operations.

It was possible to get a Mk IX off the ground, in a stiff breeze, in about fifty yards – a feat that surprised visiting USAAF P-47 Thunderbolt pilots whose large fighters required some 600 yards to take off safely. The Spitfire, with its low weight-to-power ratio, developed as a useful close-support fighter-bomber, and in which role it spent much of its operational flying time over France. Its speed made it very difficult to shoot down on low-level bombing missions and, once the bombs had been dropped, the LF IX was more than a match for intercepting German fighters.

Judging by battle reports, Spitfire IXs acquitted themselves well against the vaunted Fw 190s although there were instances on both sides where individual pilots' flying and shooting ability was superior when fighting against unskilled pilots. The following experience of one pilot, whose ability must have been above average, suggests that the Mk IX was superior to the Fw 190 – certainly at the LF's optimum altitude. His squadron was escorting US Marauder medium bombers on a raid to Woensdrecht and they were turned back, because of cloud, over Walcheren, where more than a dozen Fw 190s attacked from above, shooting down one of the Spitfires in the first rush. The squadron broke up and what happened to its leader is described in the official history:

'He [Squadron Leader D G Andrews] was subjected to repeated attacks from ahead, beam and astern which

Top left: DP 845, one of two special Spitfires used by Rolls-Royce as an engine test bed, here testing a Griffon III *Left:* The man sitting on the wing guides the pilot of a French Spitfire IX onto a snow covered runway

damaged his Spitfire in several places and put the radio-telephone out of action. Unable to call for help, Andrews lost height almost to ground level near Walcheren in an attempt to shake off his pursuers, though he now had to face ground fire as well. Gradually the number of enemy aircraft decreased until only four remained attacking the Spitfire, which was making little homeward progress due to the necessity of continually breaking away from the enemy. Up to this point Andrews had had no opportunity to fire his guns, but by the time he was ten miles west of Walcheren, having shaken off another two Focke-Wulfs, he was in a position to turn against the weakening attackers. This unexpected offensive move caused one of the enemy to run directly into his concentrated fire. A lucky bullet must have killed the German pilot for this aircraft immediately dived into the sea with a tremendous splash and the remaining Focke-Wulfs then hurried away at full speed, allowing Andrews to return to Manston.'

German fighter pilots considered it wise to adopt ambush techniques against the Mk IXs and often used a couple of Me 109s as decoys which, when attacked, would run for France where Fw 190s waited in cloud until the Spitfires were positioned beneath them and would then dive for a quick kill. If they spotted the Germans in time, the Spitfire pilots would take violent evasive action and, by using emergency power, could escape the trap. Towards the end of 1943 many of the now numerous Spitfire squadrons had been equipped with Mk IXs and, as all squadrons were by now overstaffed, there was relative inactivity for their pilots. Routine duties for Mk IXs were sweeps, bomber escorts, defence and convoy patrols. A simulated seaborne invasion that moved to within sight of the coast of the Pas-de-Calais, laid on to test the Luftwaffe defences, failed to bring up hordes of enemy fighters and only two were brought down during the whole of the operation; the Germans were unwilling to risk their main defence forces against RAF and USAAF air supremacy, which was overwhelming and thus rarely challenged. In one

Spitfire LF IXs on dispersal on
an airstrip in Yugoslavia

Spitfire IXCs in a wintry setting on the south coast of England

action that took place on 8th October, a Spitfire squadron shot down five out of eight Me 110s, two Spitfires being lost and one pilot killed. Pilots developed a dislike for attacking ground targets where enemy flak was thick and accurate, preferring the risks of enemy guns in aerial combat.

Attacking V1 flying bomb sites resulted in the loss of many Hurri-bombers and bomb-equipped Spitfires; Mk IX pilots preferred to tackle the V1s in the air but this sport was for faster types. One Mk IX pilot was flying near the Hague when he saw a V2 rocket wobbling from its launching pad into the air at a few miles per hour. As he approached to fire his cannon into the monster it quickly gained terrific speed and shot up past the Spitfire, the blast rocking the plane from a distance of a couple of hundred yards.

From December 1943 to when the first V1 pilotless flying bomb crossed the Channel on the night of 12th June 1944, some 5,000 tons of bombs and explosives were dropped by heavy and medium bombers, and rocket-firing Hurricanes and Spitfires. The first Spitfire bombing raid was made in April on Bouillancourt V1 sites which

were surrounded by batteries of 88mm, 37mm and 20mm flak guns. The Spitfire pilots had practised their own style of dive-bombing and a few were accurate enough to drop their bombs within a 100-foot diameter circle. They flew directly towards the target and when it had passed from sight under the leading edge of their wings, dived at over 400 mph down to 3,000 feet, pulled back on the stick, counted four and let go their 500-pounders. Jinking from side to side, heads down in an instinctive posture against flak, they left at full bore without bothering to turn to gloat over direct hits, if any. Checking results was left to PR Spitfires and other aircraft with cameras. During this period, Germany and vital areas in Occupied Europe were being softened up by the Allied air forces, and emergency bombers of the inaccurate Spitfire type were welcome to add their weight to the attacks on V1 sites. As fighter-bombers, Spitfires were also engaged in the pre-D-Day attacks on German defences along the Normandy coast.

Fighter superiority was essential for the success of the climactic Operation 'Overlord' which began on 6th June. Much of the air fighting and

Crews work on Spitfires operating in support of the Allied invasion of southern France in 1944.

attacks on enemy airfields, aircraft factories and oilfields in 1943–44 checked and reduced Germany's fighter strength. A special operation, 'Pointblank', had been planned to achieve this end; German aircraft production was reduced by about sixty per cent, and from November 1943 to June 1944 over 5,000 enemy aircraft were destroyed in battle, taking with them many experienced pilots.

Just before D-Day, Allied aircraft were painted with black and white stripes around fuselages and wings to facilitate easy recognition in the crowded air over the Channel and France. Within four days of the landing on Normandy a wing of Canadian Spitfires was operating from a French airfield, so dusty that Vokes filters had to be fitted. Thirty squadrons of Spitfires were based in France by the end of June, flying from airfields and landing strips where refuelling and rearming facilities were provided, and there were short, narrow strips for emergency belly-landings. With large fighter forces designated for the war in Western Europe operating from British airfields, the Air Ministry changed Fighter Command's title, for the sake of simplicity, back to Air Defence of Great Britain – ADGB.

After the invasion, pilots were instructed to shoot up anything mechanical that moved on the roads and in one such action Field-Marshal Rommel's staff car was attacked by a Spitfire IX; after one burst from the Spitfire's guns and cannon the car overturned and Rommel's skull was fractured. Thousands of sorties were flown by Mk IXs supporting the assault on Caen and, with other aircraft of the Second Tactical Air Force and ADGB, they strafed and bombed ahead of the armies, destroying 400 tanks, 4,000 other vehicles and 260 barges in the month of August alone. In the operations which culminated in the Allied landing between Toulon and Nice, Operation 'Anvil', Mk IXs were part of the Allied Mediterranean Air Force which gave excellent close support to the armies and cleared the skies of enemy fighters and bombers. Mk IXs also operated over Corsica and were later the first Allied aircraft to land at Hassani airfield near Athens.

The next two Spitfire marks were both PR models, the Marks X and XI, described in the section on PR Spitfires.

Griffon, photo-reconnaissance and floatplanes

Another development of the Rolls-Royce 'R', which powered the Supermarine S.6/6A/6B, was the '37', built in 1939 and with the same bore, six inches, and stroke, six and a half inches; it had a larger frontal area than the Merlin but this was reduced to 7.9 square feet so that it could be adapted for use in the Spitfire. The new engine was named Griffon, after the mythical bird, and in its first three marks – IIB, III and IV – gave 1,735 hp and weighed 1,980 pounds.

The first Griffon was installed in a Spitfire Mk IV prototype, which was later designated Mk XX to avoid confusion with the Merlin-powered PR IV. An order for a production run of 750 Mk IVs was cancelled and it was not until 1942 that 100 Spitfires were converted to Griffon engines. Mk Vs, already converted to Mk IX standard while still in the contract stage, together with Mk VIIIs still on the production lines, were converted into Mk XIIs by fitting Griffon engines with their attendant equipment, for the prime purpose of chasing the Fw 190s, with derated low-altitude engines, which were making sneak

raids across the Channel. The Mk XII was an interim type until the advent of the Mk XIV (which was still something of an interim type) and the 'super-Spitfire', the Mk XVIII. The Mk XII was given extra length and more strengthening in the fuselage to take the extra weight and power of the Griffon. As a result of the greater frontal area of the Griffon, the engine cowling had to be given two pronounced bulges to cover the cylinder banks. The propeller fitted was a four-blade Rotol with Jablo or Dural blades. The Griffon engine rotated in the opposite direction to the Merlin, and this produced a strong swing to the right on take-off compared with the left-hand swing associated with the Merlin. About half of the Mk XIIs produced had retractable tail-wheels, this being dependent on whether the particular aircraft was converted from Mk V/IX or Mk VIII standard. The wings of Mk XIIs were always clipped as they were used only in the low altitude role, an armament was similar to that of the Mk IX and the Mk VIII. It had a fast maximum cruising speed of 364 mph but a short range of 329 miles at

economical cruising. After take-off, the Mk XII could reach 5,000 feet in little over a minute but took 6.7 minutes to reach 20,000 feet. At 5,500 feet its maximum speed was 372 mph and at 18,000 feet, 393 mph.

With the potentially more powerful Griffon available, Supermarine made preliminary plans for a new aircraft, to be called Spiteful, with new wings of laminar-flow type. However, the demands of war made it necessary to shelve the plans and several more Spitfire types were built instead. Thus the Mk XIII only got as far as its basic airframe, borrowed from several Mk VIIIs, the airframe type also used in the construction of the Mk XIV which was the next production Griffon-engined Spitfire, 957 of the type being built, the first couple of dozen entering service with No 610 Squadron in January 1944.

The most distinguishing feature of the Mk XIV was the five-blade Rotol airscrew which was driven by a Griffon 65 of 2,035 hp. The 'E' wing was fitted to most models and a few also had cut-down rear fuselages and all-round vision cockpit canopies. The Mk XIV

Spitfire XII – the first production mark to utilise the Griffon engine

had a maximum speed of 448 mph at 26,000 feet and 417 mph at 12,000 feet. It was a very fast aircraft indeed and was the first fighter to shoot down an Me 262 turbojet-powered fighter in combat; this happened on 5th October 1944. The Mk XIV had a service ceiling of 44,500 feet and a range, with auxiliary fuel, of 850 miles at an economical cruising speed of 245 mph. Its weight varied between 6,510 pounds empty and 8,600 pounds fully armed and fuelled.

As the V1 'doodle-bug' menace continued to speed across from the Continent in 1944, a frantic effort was made to stop them from hitting London by combining all the resources of the defences. It was not long after the four that fell on the first night – including one on London's Bethnal Green suburb – that the numbers rapidly increased until 2,000 of Hitler's 'Vengeance' weapons had been launched. The death roll by 1st July was over 2,500 in south-east England, most of them in London.

To combat the menace an extensive balloon barrage was floated in rows on the south-east approaches to the city, hundreds of anti-aircraft guns of all calibres were scattered around the coast where the V1s crossed at heights varying from 3,000 to 4,000 feet, and the fastest fighters were set to patrol the Channel and the inland area behind coastal guns. Carrying rather less than a ton of explosive as their warhead, the V1s crossed the coast at about 340 mph increasing to about 400 mph by the time they reached London. Pilots attacking them were told not to fire at less than 200 yards from directly behind or they would risk having their planes destroyed when the bomb exploded: the safest way was to allow the V1 to fly past on one side then shoot it down, allowing for a slight deflection from about 200 yards: by flying just in front of the V1 its flight could be spoiled by an aircraft's swirling slipstream . thus causing it to crash; another method was to fly alongside the V1, place a wingtip under the wingtip of the V1 and quickly bank away, causing the V1 to spin to the ground.

The V1 operations employed Spitfires, Typhoons, Tempests, Mosquitoes and Mustangs, patrols being maintained at heights above the expected trajectories so that extra speed could be built up in the dive to intercept. Of the Spitfires, cropped Mk IXs and Griffon-engined Mk XIIs and XIVs were fast enough for this purpose, although to give them extra speed, armour was removed, wings and fuselages were highly polished and some motors were extravagantly boosted. Spitfires shot down scores of V1s during the months that the attack lasted.

There was no Mk XV Spitfire, the mark number being used as a Seafire designation. And the next mark, the XVI, was basically a Mk IX using a Packard-built Merlin 66 – the 266 of 1,580 hp. Equipped with 'E' wings – some had 'C' wings – the 1,054 Mk XVIs served primarily as ground attack fighters, coming into service late in 1944. Early in 1945 the Mk XVIs were given all-around vision canopies and cut-down rear fuselages. Another difference was that this type had an additional rear fuselage tank

for extra range on long ferrying flights; otherwise the performance and other data of the Mk IX applied to the Mk XVI.

Finally war service in Europe came to an end for Spitfires. With invasion from the West and from the East, Germany collapsed, with her air power dissipated and eventually destroyed on the ground more than in the air. The war in the Far East continued and Spitfires were developed for further operations there but the principal type, the Mk XVIII, arrived too late and the action was left to Seafires. The designation Mk XVII was reserved for Seafires and other Spitfire progress ended with the F24. By then the fighter's appearance had changed considerably and the characteristic wing shape was redesigned from elliptical to a more tapered shape on the F21.

There was already a marked difference in the long nosed Griffon-engined Spitfires with five-blade propellers and the Mk XVIII was the last development of the original airframe; it was strengthened in fuselage and undercarriage to allow for the extra weight of twenty-six-and-a-half gallons of fuel in the wings and sixty-six gallons in the rear fuselage. The Mk XVIII was really a consolidated Mk XIV, although only one hundred of the later Mk XVIIIs were built as fighters and 200 as fighter-reconnaissance aircraft. The Mk XVIII did see service in postwar years as a strike aircraft in Malaya against Communist guerillas. The Mk XIX was a PR aircraft.

The Mk VIII was the first major aerodynamic redesign of the basic Spitfire and the F21 the second and final one. The F21 was produced when machine guns had been outmoded and its new wings, blunter at the tips and equipped with trimming tabs on ailerons, contained four cannon and carried rockets and bombs. It was nevertheless a handsome aircraft, and went into service at the end of 1945. Powered by the 2,050 hp Griffon 61, the F21's maximum speed was 450 mph at heights from

Vickers Supermarine Spitfire FR XIVE (6 Squadron RIAF 1946)
Engine: Rolls-Royce Griffon 65 or 66, 2,035 hp *Armament:* Two 20mm
Hispano Mk II cannon with 120 rounds per gun and two .5-inch Browning
machine guns with 250 rounds per gun, plus one 500 lb and two 250 lb bombs
Maximum speed: 448 mph at 26,000 feet *Initial climb rate:* 4,580 feet per minute
Ceiling: 44,500 feet *Range:* 460 miles normal, 850 miles max
Weight empty: 6,510 lbs *Weight loaded:* 8,600 lbs *Span:* 36 feet 10 inches
Length: 32 feet 10 inches

Spitfire F 21s

19,000 to 26,000 feet, 420 mph at 12,000 feet and 390 mph at sea level. Its internal fuel capacity of 120 gallons (the wings each holding one eighteen-gallon tank) gave it a range of 490 miles at 285 mph, range being boosted to 880 miles with maximum auxiliary fuel. One hundred and twenty F21s were built before production was cancelled with the cessation of hostilities. A slightly different model, the F22, was also built at the same time with 260 coming off the assembly lines before cancellation of the order. The only differences between the two aircraft were the redesigned all-round vision canopy and cut down fuselage of the F22, and a 24 volt electrical system instead of the F21's 12 volt system.

In 1946 the last Spitfire entered RAF service and in 1948 the last Spitfire, an

Left: **Postwar photograph of an F 21**
Below left: **Originally ordered as Mk IXs, these F 21s display to advantage the later broad-chord fin and rudder and bubble canopy**
Below: **An immaculate example of the F 24 series**

F24, was built. The F24 was a modified F22 and only eighty-one were built; sixteen were eventually sent to Hong Kong and, in 1952, twenty-four were mothballed but were later scrapped. In these last Griffon-engined models the Spitfire was as perfect as it could possibly be developed in its form as an interceptor fighter. In the ten years after the first Spitfire went into service in 1938, 20,334 were built, as well as 2,408 Seafires.

Another special need encountered during the Second World War was for accurate and speedy reconnaissance so that any situation could be evaluated and acted upon with the minimum of delay.

The essential qualities of a photo-reconnaissance aircraft during the Second World War were high altitude flight and speed, to give it immunity from enemy interceptors, and range. All combatants built aircraft of this type, improvising until the ideal twin-engined aircraft could evolve from their aeronautical resources. Ideally, a PR aircraft required the services of both pilot and navigator for accurate flights over long distances at

heights where strong winds might often cause reconnaissance flights to drift wide of the target.

Early in the war Britain had only one fast high-flying aircraft for this purpose and its range was restricted: Spitfire Is were first stripped of armour and armament and sent, in 1940, to PR stations in France, carrying cameras in the chute positions in the fuselage behind the cockpit. Spitfire conversions to the PR role were known as series A to G, which reached a high degree of development in the type known as the PR 'D'. This aircraft was given an extra fuel capacity of 133 gallons by fitting tanks internally along the wing leading edges. From this model evolved the Spitfire PR IV (Supermarine Type 353), based on the Mk V airframe, of which 229 were built to serve, from 1942, in five special squadrons.

To remain immune from interception, PR aircraft had to fly at least as high as 40,000 feet where not only was the cold intense, but the lowering of the atmospheric pressure produced also an adverse physical effect on pilots, causing them some pain when they flew at this height for long periods: a small pressure cabin built into the cockpit was developed at the Royal Aircraft Establishment and was tested in a Merlin 4-engined Mk V in 1941. These pressure cabins were fitted as standard in the elongated-wing Spitfires HF VI and VII, which were designed to destroy enemy PR aircraft by their ability to climb to a higher altitude and still be able to perform as satisfactory fighters.

The PR VII was also a modified Mk V (and not a modified HF VII) and was originally known as the PR 'G'. Unlike its predecessors it carried no radio but was armed with machine guns and was also armoured. Its PR functions were for lower altitudes and its cameras were a vertical F24 with 5 inch lens or one vertical and one oblique F24 with 14 inch lens.

The PR XI was the Mk IX converted for photographic work, the conversion being made at the RAF station at Benson; they were the only Mk IXs to be given retractable tailwheels. With a Merlin 70, this PR aircraft had a maximum speed of 422 mph at 27,500 feet, a service ceiling of 44,000

feet, a range of 1,360 miles and could climb to 20,000 feet in five minutes. Its radio was either the standard TR 1133 or the TR1143 with beam approach equipment. For weight considerations the cockpit was not pressurised except on a variant of the type designated PRX, of which sixteen were built. The USAAF received eight PR XIs of which a total of 471 were built, 309 of them tropicalised.

After the introduction of the Griffon engines, two improved Fighter Reconnaissance (FR) types were produced: the FR XIV and FR XVIII were both fully-armed fighters and carried an oblique F24 camera in the fuselage. The next purely PR model was the PR XIX, first delivered in May 1944, fully pressurised and powered by the Griffon 66 of 2,035 hp. 225 of this type were built, thirty of them unpressurised. Empty, the aircraft weighed 6,520 pounds and loaded, 9,202 pounds. With its leading-edge tanks and a 170-gallon drop-tank filled, its overload weight rose to 10,450 pounds, but it could still get off to fly 1,500 miles at 35,000 feet. Its stalling speed with this load was 95 mph. Maximum speed was 446 mph at 26,000 feet and 360 mph at sea-level, and service ceiling was 42,000 feet. The aircraft carried two vertical F52 fanned cameras with 20 or 36 inch lens, and two vertical F8s with 20 inch lens, or two fanned F24s with 14 inch lens and an oblique F24 with 8 or 14 inch lens. A Type K dinghy was carried in this and other PR Spitfires.

There were of course many other types of RAF aircraft in operation as PR types during the war, flying under the control of Coastal Command. The Benson station became headquarters for operational and development work which mostly benefitted Bomber Command, who required before-and-after pictures of targets. Two complex and vital PR jobs were done for D-Day planning and Operation 'No-ball' – the attacks on the V1 flying bomb sites.

Right: The development of
Photographic Reconaissance
Spitfires *Top:* PR IV of September 1941
Centre: PR XIII of early 1943
Bottom: Earlier in mark number than
the previous but later in service –
the Spitfire PR X

General Eisenhower ordered a complete photographic coverage of the invasion beaches and hinterland of Normandy for the building of relief maps. Oblique shots from just above sea-level at high and at low tide gave invasion barge and landing-craft coxswains a preview of their landing points, and enabled battalion commanders to visualise the terrain where their troops would fight. Photographs assisted engineers concerned with airfields, bridges, roads, depots and underwater obstacles off the beaches. On one day alone, 6th June, over 450 reconnaissance sorties were flown over these areas.

Reports from secret agents in France and aerial reconnaissance photographs formed the evidence that confirmed the existence of Hitler's flying-bomb weapon. The pinpointing of the many actual and possible sites, and the activities surrounding the V2 rocket sites, occupied forty per cent of Allied PR sorties and more than 4,000,000 prints were made from 1,250,000 negatives taken in the period of ten months from May 1943.

Another special adaptation brought about by the special circumstances of the Second World War was engendered by the need for a fighter capable of operating from any available space in a country lacking many airfields.

For an aircraft that took to the sea more like a fish than a buoyant seagull, floating above the water was a strange but successful conversion that produced, in its Mk IX version, the war's fastest floatplane. The first Spitfire floatplane was a conversion of a Mk I, and was produced at the time of the German invasion of Norway, when it was feared that the insufficiency of suitable airfields in that country would hinder the support that the RAF could otherwise give to the army. Thus there emerged a requirement for a fighter capable of flying from the fjords which abound on the coast of Norway. In the interests of speed, floats from a Blackburn Roc

were fitted to a Spitfire I, but tests were not successful. As the campaign for which the conversion was needed was rapidly drawing to a close, further tests were not made.

The idea was revived, however, with the beginning of the war in the Pacific against Japan, when it was realised that a floatplane fighter with good performance would be an invaluable asset in the island campaigns which seemed likely in this theatre. It was decided to try the Spitfire again, and Folland Aircraft Ltd undertook the conversion to the Type 335 of a Mk VB and a set of Supermarine-designed floats. The combination proved to be an immediate success. In the Mk VB floatplane, the carburettor air intake was extended to avoid spray, a propeller with four shorter blades was fitted to the Merlin, cantilever pylons attached the floats to the inboard wing sections, a ventral fin replaced the tailwheel and the fin was extended slightly forward to increase the vertical tail surface area.

When a Spitfire was throttled back there was a yawing effect and this was increased in the floatplane – otherwise its manoeuvrability was very good. Folland built several sets of floats and converted another two Mk Vs, one of which served in the Mediterranean, before converting a Mk IX powered by a Merlin 45. This aircraft had a maximum speed of 377 mph at 19,700 feet and a service ceiling of 36,000 feet. With a fifty gallon drop tank, the Mk IX floatplane had a range of 770 miles at 225 mph at 10,000 feet. As an armed reconnaissance aircraft the Mk IX floatplane would have been very useful in the Pacific area where the Japanese operated several monoplane and biplane types, all two-seaters except two Zero-type conversions, Rex and Rufe. Rex was the better performer, built in 1942 but not produced in any great number until towards the end of 1943. Its top speed was 302 mph at 18,700 feet, service ceiling 34,600 feet, range 1,036 miles, and it was armed with two 7.7mm machine guns and two 20mm cannon. The Rex was probably more manoeuvrable than the Spitfire IX floatplane which would thus have had to rely on speed in any mix-up with the Japanese aircraft.

Seafire, Spiteful and Seafang

Spitfires joined the Navy as carrier aircraft when the Admiralty gave their approval, in 1941, after Sea-Hurricanes had demonstrated that aircraft with fast landing speeds could operate safely from carrier decks. A strong point in favour of the Spitfire was that if it did stall a few feet above the deck, it would still come down tamely.

The first Fleet Air Arm carrier-landing Spitfires were fitted with arrester gear, instruments calibrated in knots and lugs fitted for lashing and slinging. They were called 'hooked Spitfires' at first, then Seafires; forty-eight of them – Mk VBs – were converted by Air Services Training Ltd at Hamble, in 1942, as Seafire IBs. Commander H P Bramwell test-landed the first Seafire on a carrier, HMS *Illustrious*, and the first FAA squadron to be equipped with the Seafire IB was No 807. Air Service Training, Supermarine and Cunliffe-Owen Aircraft produced 188 Seafire IBs which had a performance similar to the RAF type. They carried a Type K dinghy, TR 1196 or TR 1304 transmitter/receiver and a Type G 45 cine camera installed in the wing-root. Because the wings did not fold, the aircraft could not be carried down in the lifts of carriers to hangar decks.

This navalised Spitfire flew into action for the first time off HMS *Furious* during Operation 'Torch' off French North Africa escorting Fairey Albacores in low-flying attacks on airfields. The first victory in the air was against a French Dewoitine D 520 shot down by Sub-Lieutenant G C Baldwin. The next important action involving FAA Seafires was in support of the Allied landing in the Gulf of Salerno in September 1943. These Seafires included 'C'-wing L IICs ('L' was the FAA equivalent of the RAF's LF) and all were fitted with the provision for RATOG (Rocket Assisted Take Off Gear). 402 Seafire IICs were built by Supermarine and Westland. Merlins 45 and 46 were the standard engines for the first two types but some were fitted with Merlins 50, 55, 56 or 32.

The next mark, Seafire III, was

Right: A fine study of a Royal Navy Seafire III doing a vertical right bank

Vickers Supermarine Spitfire F21 (91 Squadron, September 1946)
Engine: Rolls-Royce Griffon 61, 2,050 hp *Armament:* Four 20mm Hispano
Mk II cannon with 150 rounds per gun outboard and 175 rounds per gun inboard,
plus one 500 lbs and two 250 lbs bombs *Maximum speed:* 450 mph at 19,000 feet
Maximum climb rate: 4,900 feet per minute *Ceiling:* 43,00 feet *Range:* 490 miles
normal, 880 miles max *Weight empty:* 7,160 lbs *Weight loaded:* 9,900 lbs
Span: 36 feet 11 inches *Length:* 32 feet 8 inches

better equipped for stowage in that its wings folded upwards outboard of the wheel-wells and the wingtips were hinged to fold down. Westland and Cunliffe-Owen produced 1,200 Seafire IIIs in LF or L versions powered by Merlin 55M and 32 engines and F versions powered by Merlin 55s. Fighter-Reconnaissance Seafires carried one vertical and one oblique camera in the fuselage.

By the end of 1942 there were six FAA squadrons equipped with Seafires, another six were equipped by the end of 1943 and there were also several Seafires attached to four squadrons flying other aircraft off escort carriers. FAA squadrons operated with the Desert Air Force and were in action on D-Day. Early in 1945 the Royal Navy began operations in the Far East, collaborating with the large US task forces that ranged the Pacific from the Philippines to Japan itself. Eight squadrons of Seafire IIIs, in the fleet carriers *Implacable* and *Indefatigable* and the escort carriers *Hunter, Stalker, Attacker* and *Chaser*, joined squadrons of Avengers and Fireflies attacking Japanese oil refineries in Sumatra. Another raid by a task force, which included HMS *Illustrious* and USS *Saratoga*, destroyed twenty-four Japanese aircraft, set oil tanks on fire, bombed airfields and sank a ship, without loss of any British or American aircraft. The FAA also operated over Sakishima Island, the large enemy base at Truk and, in August, on the wide shooting sweeps over the Japanese Home Islands. Seafires also covered the invasions of Rangoon and Penang.

Construction of the Griffon-engined Seafire had begun at Westland and Cunliffe-Owen but the F XV went into service too late for the Second World War. A naval version of the Spitfire XII, this Seafire had an improved hook, a sting-type arrester mounted at the extreme end of the tail – accomodated by cutting away the bottom of the rudder. After the war, several were transferred to the Royal Canadian Navy, the Burmese air force and one, highly polished and stripped of paint, was a demonstration aircraft at the US Naval Test Centre.

The Mk XVII was a Mk XV with cut down rear fuselage and rear-view canopy and strengthened undercarriage. The Mk XVII stayed in service longer than any other Seafire – to November 1954. This type was followed by the F/FR 45 – a navalised version of the Spitfire F 21 – with non-folding wings. Then a copy of the Spitfire F 22, the Seafire F/FR 46, was introduced before the last of the Seafires, and the first postwar model to go into action, was built as a naval version of the Spitfire F 24. This was the Seafire F/FR 47, with folding wings but fixed tips, that flew off the light fleet carrier *Triumph* to make rocket strikes against guerrilla hideouts in Malaya in October 1949. In 1950, again flying off *Triumph*, Seafire 47s were in action during the Korean war, performing 245 offensive fighter patrols and 115 ground-attack operations. The F/FR 47 was armed with four short-barrel Hispano 20mm cannon and could carry two 250 pound bombs or eight 60-pound rockets. Maximum speed was 451 mph at 20,000 feet and, with a rear-fuselage tank of thirty-three gallons and seventy-nine gallons in a belly and two wing tanks, range was extended to 940 miles. The last Seafire, the 2,048th, was completed in March 1949.

The Spiteful was made by Vickers-Supermarine and, because it was produced as a direct development of the Spitfire, should be mentioned. Perhaps the only visual connection between the two aircraft was a profile similar to the F 24. The first prototype crashed and the second made its maiden flight in June 1944, and it was not until November 1946, that the RAF received their first four-cannon Spiteful F14s powered by 2,375 hp Griffons. Griffons 89 or 90 were installed in a second version which became the F 15, and the Griffon 101, which had a three-stage blower, powered the record-breaking F 16 which achieved 494 mph. This latter type was not included in the carrier-borne versions of the Spiteful, which were named Seafang. Nine F 31 and two F 32 Seafangs were flown by the Navy; seven others delivered were not assembled for flying operations. The RAF received 373 Spitefuls before new jet fighters relegated them to obsolescence.

Left centre: Seafire *Left:* Seafang

Epilogue

Two squadrons of Spitfire IXs in the *Armée de l'Air* were used in action by the French during their reoccupation of Indo-China and, in Indonesia, Spitfire VIIIs of No 155 Squadron, RAF were sent on strikes against extremists during the postwar troubles. Spitfires were called into action in Malaya during the attempted takeover by Communist insurgents in 1947. A South African squadron trained on Spitfire IXs before going to Korea to fly Mustangs.

Some confusion arose in the Middle East during the Israel-Egypt war of 1948, for both sides had Spitfires and so did the British who were neutral but based on Egyptian airfields. Thus Spitfires from Egypt were set against Israeli Spitfires and on one occasion four British FR XVIIIs flying a purely RAF reconnaissance mission were shot down, one by Israeli anti-aircraft fire and the others by a group of Israeli Spitfires! Three of the British pilots baled out. Israel eventually sold her Spitfires to Burma.

The last RAF operational flight by Spitfires was an attack on a Malayan terrorist hide-out in the Johore area, made by Spitfire FR XVIIIs of No 60 Squadron.

A Spitfire Fund was in existence during the war and its purpose was simply to raise money by public subscription to purchase Spitfires for the war effort. In 1940, 5,000 pounds sterling was the figure publicised as the price of a Spitfire. They actually cost a little more than this and by the end of the war the figure for an F 21 would have been at least double that of a Mk I. Hundreds were purchased from these public subscriptions and from private donations, each presentation aircraft bearing the name of the donor. For example: City of Coventry (there were three of these), Bow Street Home Guard, Sind (several of these), On The Target (from Army gunners), Cheeping Wycombe, Kalahari (Bechuanaland), The Old Lady (of Threadneedle Street), Lady Linlithgow, R J Mitchell (obviously the employees of Supermarine), Victor McLaglen – Seattle, Metal Trade – Australia, The Dog Fighter (Kennel Club), Carbine (Victoria Racing Club, Australia), Flying Scotsman (LNER), Sir Harry and Lady Oakes (two), Dorothy of Great Britain And The Empire (!), The Canadian Policeman, Queen Salote, and Prince Tungi Tonga No II. Presentation names were painted along the side of the engine cowling or below the cockpit.

Spitfires (taken over on reverse Lend-Lease) flown by the USAAF flew on 28,981 sorties, shot down 256 enemy aircraft, and dropped 202 tons of bombs. The Americans lost 191 of their Spitfires in combat.

Over 1,300 Spitfires, mostly LF IXs, were shipped to Russia where they operated in close support of ground troops. One Mk IX in Russian service shot down four Me 109s in an action reported during the fighting in the autumn of 1944.

Before sanctions to export Spitfires was withdrawn when war became imminent, Britain exported three Mk Is to Turkey. Several more Spitfires of different types were sent to Turkey after that country came to support Britain against Germany which had previously supplied the Turks with Fw 190s.

Spitfire Is and IIs were camouflaged in brown and green on the upper surfaces with light grey, green or blue underneath; some Mk Vs varied from these colours to dark green and grey on top. HF Spitfires had standard fighter camouflage paintwork and in the Middle East the HF VIIs were light blue with red and blue roundels and black squadron letters and production serial numbers.

The first two letters before the roundel denoted the code for the squadron and the letter on the other side of the roundel was its individual identity letter within the squadron. Some wing commanders and senior officers replaced squadron lettering with their own initials: Clive Caldwell's Mk VC, in natural metal finish except for a black anti-glare strip along the engine cowling, blue and white fin flash and roundels, was lettered CR-C. All British aircraft had serial numbers painted on their rear fuselage. Spitfire serials began with prototype K5054 and the last was Seafire VR972. The numbers were changed if aircraft were grounded for maintenance instruction in the RAF or if the aircraft were transferred to other countries. Normal roundel paintwork was a red centre, narrow white circle, wide blue circle and, on the outer circumference, a narrow yellow circle which gave the roundel a visual lift away from the camouflage paint. Other roundels were sometimes just red and blue, particularly for the upper wing position; roundels were painted on both sides and on top and bottom of most Spitfires. The flash on the rudder fin was normally red and blue with a thin white stripe down the centre.

A unique Mk VC was one equipped with a second cockpit, in front of the pilot's, for the use of a batman. This aircraft flew on liaison work from No 261 Squadron in Sicily. Two-seater Mk IX trainers were built for the Irish Air Corps in 1951 and other two-seaters were converted from Mk VIIIs.

When Portugal feared an invasion by pro-Nazi Spaniards in 1943, Britain shipped fifty Mk VBs to the Portuguese air force. Mk VCs left in Greece at the end of the war were taken into service by the Greeks who also purchased seventy-seven Mk IXs. The French air force added seventy Mk VBs to Spitfires retained by the Free French *Escadrille de Chasse I* after operating in the Middle East. One Mk VII was sent to New York in 1943; the USAAF also received seven Mk VIIIs, a PR XIX is on display at the Wright-Patterson base at Dayton, Ohio and other monumental Spitfires in the US are at Chicago, Colorado Springs, and Perry Airport, Hollywood.

Other countries which took Spitfires into service postwar were Holland, Italy, Czechoslovakia, Denmark, Norway, Rhodesia, Syria and Argentina, which received one.

The Germans captured and flight tested a Mk I, a Mk VB, a Mk IX and a Mk VIII. The Mk VB was also tested by them with a Me 109's DB601A engine and the results of the tests showed that with the German engine the Spitfire was more manoeuverable, climbed faster and had a higher service ceiling than the slightly faster Me 109G.

Spitfires stand as memorials at many RAF stations, including some of the famous Battle of Britain airfields, at Biggin Hill, Hornchurch, Tangmere, Hawkinge, Manston, Kenley, Turnhouse and Church Fenton. Other Spitfires are on airfields and in museums throughout the world: the Imperial War Museum in London, the War Museum at Canberra, at Ottawa, Athens, Rangoon, Paris, Singapore, Aukland, Johannesburg, Brussels, Eindhoven, Copenhagen and, in a children's playground, at Trad in Thailand.

Pierre Closterman, DSO, DFC, the French pilot who flew Spitfires in the RAF for most of the European war, described his experiences in his book, *The Big Show*. On the 'personality' of the Spitfire he wrote: 'The Spitfire ... is typically British. Temperate, a perfect compromise for all the qualities required of a fighter, ideally suited to its task of defence. An essentially reasonable piece of machinery, conceived by cool, precise brains and built by conscientious hands. The Spitfire left such an imprint on those who flew it that when they changed to other types they found it very hard to get acclimatised.'

Bibliography

Reach for the Sky Paul Brickhill (Collins, London)
The Second World War Winston S Churchill (Cassell, London)
Speeches Winston S Churchill (Cassell, London)
Secret Session Speeches Winston S Churchill (Cassell, London)
Leading the Few Basil Collier (Jarrolds, London)
The Defence of the United Kingdom Basil Collier (HMSO, London)
Eagle Day Richard Collier (Hodder and Stoughton, London)
Nine Lives Group Captain A C Deere (Hodder and Stoughton, London)
Invasion 1940 Peter Fleming (Hart-Davis, London)
The First and the Last Adolf Galland (Methuen, London. Holt, New York)
The Last Enemy Richard Hillary (Macmillan, London) US title *Falling Through Space* (Reynat and Hitchcock, New York)
Wing Leader J E Johnson (Chatto and Windus, London)
British War Production M M Postan (HMSO, London)
The Struggle for Europe Chester Wilmot (Collins, London)
The Narrow Margin D Wood & D Dempster (Hutchinson, London)
Fighter Command Air Vice-Marshal P G Wyetham (Putnam, London)
Royal Air Force 1939-1945 Vol. I Denis Richards (HMSO, London)